Betty Crocker's
DINNER IN A DISH
COOK BOOK

Illustrated by Helen Federico

GOLDEN PRESS **NEW YORK**

FIRST EDITION   FIRST PRINTING

Contents

Dear Friend,

From the first meat-and-vegetable dish prepared in a crude earthenware pot to the sophisticated packaged meals found in today's supermarkets, good cooks everywhere have praised the dinner in a dish for convenient cooking, simple service, and excellent eating.

From casserole and skillet, chafing dish and soup kettle come these complete and delicious dinners—satisfying and nourishing—to make families happy and parties memorable, to save you work, time, and dishwashing.

What more could you ask of any recipe? And here from the Betty Crocker Kitchens are more than 250 such recipes, dinners in a dish to serve on every occasion. To most you need add only a salad and dessert, perhaps a bread, for a well-rounded menu. As a special bonus, you'll find an information-packed chapter, our "Good Cooks' Guide," to give you added help with shopping, cooking and freezing methods, and that all-important problem—meal planning.

We sincerely hope this new collection of dinners in a dish will brighten your table, lighten your work, and please your family and friends.

Cordially,

Betty Crocker

P.S. All the recipes in this book have been tested for you in our kitchens at General Mills and by homemakers across the country.

Company Best

The one-dish dinner is perfect party fare! Easy to assemble at your leisure, well in advance of the dinner hour, it stream-lines preparation and simplifies service—and this is the secret of relaxed and gracious entertaining. What's more, it solves the harried hostess's problem of timing.

Are you planning a glamorous "sit-down" dinner, an in-formal buffet party, or a crowd-size club or church gather-ing? In this chapter you will find sparkling-new, unusual recipes as well as familiar classics for all Company Best occa-sions. Choose from casseroles meant for a connoisseur's pleasure, from popular duet dishes, or from exceptional yet economy-minded "quantity" meals.

Famous hostesses and fine chefs alike agree that a truly elegant oven casserole is first choice for an unforgettable dinner party. It's easy to plan a company dinner with a casserole as your pièce de résistance. Just precede the meal with an appetizer, accompany it with a simple but perfect salad, and add a hot bread if you wish. Then turn your time and talents to creating a dessert of distinction—the grand climax to a gourmet feast!

The casserole waits in the oven, out of sight and mind, while you, both cook and hostess, mingle serenely with your guests. Such a simple hostessing trick—a recipe from these pages, an easy menu, and—voilà! A party meal worthy of your loveliest table setting and most appreciative guests!

PLANNING YOUR PARTY

A meal featuring a casserole may be served conveniently either buffet style or as a "sit-down" dinner. Both ways have advantages, depending upon the number of guests and the seating space you have available.

THE BUFFET DINNER

For a party that almost "gives itself," choose to serve buffet style. It's informal and effortless . . . and the best way to show off your casserole masterpiece. At such a party, your success as a hostess depends on careful planning and casual service. Your reward will be a problem-free evening and contented guests who are eager to be invited again.

THE FOOD—Elegant, delicious, plentiful.

• Choose any casserole recipe from this chapter. Then complete your party menu with a compatible salad, bread, dessert, and coffee. Plan few dishes, but a bountiful quantity of each. (It is wise to hold a second casserole in reserve in a slow oven so second servings will be as appetizing as the first.)

• Be sure both casserole and bread arrive at the buffet table fragrantly hot and that the salad, perfectly chilled, comes directly from the refrigerator.

• Trim your casserole with colorful and edible garnishes—they have so much guest appeal! And add a grace note or two to your buffet table with pretty dishes of tart relish, pickled peaches, butter balls or curls.

THE DISH—Colorful, interesting, ample in size.

• Baking dishes, casseroles, skillets, chafing dishes, tureens, and platters come in such an array of glowing colors, interesting shapes, and gleaming glazes that every hostess should make her own collection of them for future party-giving. Select the one most appropriate to the food it will contain and which harmonizes best with your linen and centerpiece. Make sure it is sufficiently large to contain the food and allow guests to serve themselves without unsightly spills.

THE BUFFET TABLE—Beautiful, lavish, convenient.

• Burnished brass and copper or polished silver accessories in the glow of candlelight are lovely accents for your table. A few flowers with masses of greenery or a lavish tray of brilliant fruits or fresh vegetables makes a striking and practical centerpiece.

• Order of logical service is the simplest guide to setting a buffet table: first a stack of plates, then the main-dish casserole set at one end for added drama, followed by salad, bread and relishes, napkins and silver. (If not to be offered elsewhere, be sure to have salt and pepper shakers on the table.)

THE HOSTESS AND GUESTS—Happy and relaxed.

• Invite your guests to serve themselves. Everyone enjoys admiring your table and food, and guests feel more at ease in the group when occupied.

• You may have your dining table or several small tables for four completely set with linen, silver, and incidental service; or you may let guests carry napkins and silver with their plates to individual folding trays or tables in the living room. If you have completely set tables, coffee cups may be in place at the right of each dinner setting. Filled water glasses are passed after guests are seated.

• While your guests serve themselves, you can clear away the appetizer course. Ask guests to return to the buffet table as often as they wish, or pass the serving dishes to them. Be certain the coffee is hot and poured often. Clear all serving dishes and plates before the dessert course.

• If your dessert is especially impressive, be sure to bring it into the room and serve from the buffet or another table.

Easy, isn't it? Follow this simple plan for a delightful evening that guests and hostess alike will enjoy.

THE "SIT-DOWN" DINNER

A small group may also be entertained graciously at a "sit-down" dinner. If you wish, begin the meal with an appetizer course served in the living room.

TABLE AND SERVICE—Informal and pleasant.

• The guests are seated at a single table which has been completely set. Bread, butter, and relishes may be on the table at the beginning of the meal but removed before the dessert course.

• The casserole main dish and a stack of warmed plates are placed before the host, who serves each guest, passing the filled plates to his left.

• Salad, dessert, and coffee are usually served by the hostess, who passes them to her left.

BREAST OF CHICKEN ON RICE

The simplest party meal in the world! Serve with a big dewy green salad and butterflake rolls; follow with a glamorous ice-cream bombe or pie.

1 can (10½ oz.) cream of mushroom soup
1 soup can milk
¾ cup uncooked regular rice
1 can (4 oz.) mushroom stems and pieces
1 envelope (1½ oz.) dehydrated onion soup mix
2 chicken breasts, split in half

Heat oven to 350°. Mix mushroom soup with milk; reserve ½ cup of the mixture. Mix remaining soup mixture with rice, mushrooms (including liquid), and half of the onion soup mix. Pour into oblong baking dish, 11½x7½x1½". Place chicken breasts on top. Pour reserved soup mixture over chicken breasts; sprinkle with remaining onion soup mix. Cover and bake 1 hr.; uncover and bake 15 min. longer. *4 servings.*

CHICKEN SORRENTO

Delicious with hot biscuits and a colorful fruit salad in lettuce cups.

3 tbsp. flour
1 tsp. salt
⅛ tsp. pepper
1 tsp. parsley flakes
3 chicken breasts, split
¼ cup shortening
1 can (4 oz.) mushroom stems and pieces, drained
1 can (10½ oz.) cream of celery soup
1 tsp. crushed oregano
2 cups dairy sour cream
4 oz. elbow macaroni, cooked and drained
1 pkg. (10 oz.) frozen green peas, thawed
Paprika

Heat oven to 350°. Mix flour, salt, pepper, and parsley flakes; coat chicken breasts with this mixture. Brown in hot shortening; remove from skillet. Add mushrooms to skillet; cook and stir about 5 min. Drain off excess fat. Stir in soup and oregano until smooth. Remove from heat; stir in sour cream. Place macaroni in oblong baking dish, 11½x7½x1½". With a fork, lightly mix in peas and *half* the soup mixture. Arrange chicken breasts on top; pour remaining soup mixture over chicken. Sprinkle with paprika. Cover and bake 40 min.; uncover and bake 20 min. longer. *6 servings.*

MAI KAI CHICKEN

1 can (1 lb. 4 oz.) sliced
   pineapple, drained
   (reserve ⅓ cup syrup)
¼ cup soy sauce
2 tsp. ground ginger
¼ tsp. pepper
2½- to 3-lb. broiler-fryer
   chicken, cut up

½ cup Gold Medal Flour
   (regular or Wondra)
¼ cup shortening
3 cups cooked rice
¾ cup raisins
¼ cup toasted diced
   almonds
Curry Sauce (below)

Combine reserved pineapple syrup, soy sauce, ginger, and pepper. Place chicken in large dish; pour pineapple marinade over pieces. Place in refrigerator 1 hr. Turn chicken pieces and marinate 1 hr. longer. Remove chicken and reserve the marinade. Shake chicken in paper bag with flour. Brown thoroughly in hot shortening, about 20 min.

Heat oven to 350°. Combine rice, raisins, and almonds in oblong baking dish, 11½x7½x1½″. Place pineapple slices over rice mixture. Top with browned chicken; sprinkle chicken with 3 tbsp. of the reserved marinade. Cover and bake 40 min.; uncover and bake 10 min. longer, or until chicken is done. Serve with Curry Sauce. *4 servings.*

CURRY SAUCE

1 tbsp. butter or margarine
1 tbsp. flour
1 tbsp. instant minced
   onion
⅛ tsp. garlic powder

½ tsp. curry powder
¼ tsp. ground ginger
1 cup milk
¼ cup toasted coconut

Melt butter over low heat in heavy saucepan. Stir in flour, onion, garlic powder, curry powder, and ginger. Cook, stirring until mixture is bubbly. Remove from heat. Stir in milk. Heat to boiling, stirring constantly. Boil 1 min. Stir in coconut; heat.

TURKEY DIVAN

¼ cup butter or margarine
¼ cup Gold Medal Flour
   (regular or Wondra)
1½ cups chicken broth*
2 tbsp. sherry
⅛ tsp. nutmeg
½ cup whipping cream,
   whipped
½ cup grated Parmesan
   cheese

1½ lb. fresh broccoli,
   cleaned, cooked, and
   drained, or 2 pkg. (10
   oz. each) frozen broc-
   coli spears, cooked
   and drained
5 large slices cooked
   turkey or chicken
   breast meat (about
   ¾ lb.)
½ cup grated Parmesan
   cheese

In a heavy saucepan, melt butter over low heat. Blend in flour. Cook over low heat, stirring until smooth and bubbly. Remove from heat. Gradually stir in broth. Heat to boiling, stirring constantly. Boil 1 min. Remove from heat. Stir in sherry and nutmeg; gently fold in whipped cream and ½ cup cheese. Place the hot broccoli in baking dish, 11½x 7½x1½″; top with large slices of turkey. Pour sauce over meat. Sprinkle with ½ cup cheese. Set oven control at "broil." Broil 3 to 5″ from heat until cheese is bubbly and lightly browned. *5 servings.*

*Chicken broth may be made by dissolving 1 chicken bouillon cubes in 1½ cups boiling water, or use canned chicken broth.

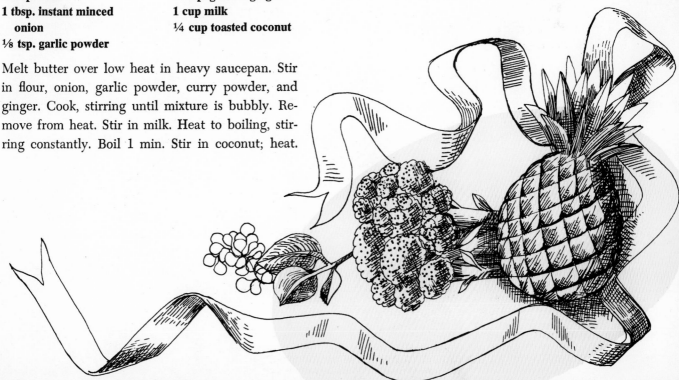

LOBSTER ÉLÉGANTE

Chunks of pink lobster on a bed of pale-green spinach noodles, all topped with a luscious gourmet sauce. Serve with cantaloupe-strawberry salads when in season; other times, pass a tray of sparkling melon pickles. Pictured opposite.

¼ cup minced onion	¼ cup sherry
2 tbsp. butter or margarine	4 oz. spinach egg noodles (green), cooked and drained*
2 tbsp. flour	
½ tsp. salt	
¼ tsp. pepper	2 cups cubed cooked lobster meat
¼ tsp. dry mustard	
1½ cups milk	2 tbsp. lemon juice
1 cup shredded process American cheese	½ cup shredded process American cheese

Heat oven to 375°. Cook and stir onion in butter until tender; remove from heat. Blend in flour and seasonings. Cook over low heat, stirring until mixture is bubbly. Remove from heat. Stir in milk. Heat to boiling, stirring constantly. Boil 1 min. Add 1 cup cheese; stir over low heat until melted. Stir in sherry. Arrange cooked noodles around sides of oblong baking dish, 10x6x1½″; place cubed lobster in center and sprinkle with lemon juice. Pour sauce over noodles and lobster and sprinkle with ½ cup shredded cheese. Bake 25 min., or until mixture is bubbly and lightly browned. Garnish with twists of lemon, if desired. *4 to 5 servings.*

*Spinach egg noodles may be cooked by the same method as other noodles. Follow package directions or see p. 142.

LOBSTER EN COQUILLE

4 frozen lobster tails (5 to 8 oz. each)	2 tbsp. butter, melted
	½ tsp. grated lemon peel
1 pkg. of our noodles Romanoff	1 tbsp. lemon juice
1 tsp. monosodium glutamate	1 pkg. (9 oz.) frozen artichoke hearts, cooked and drained
½ tsp. salt	Paprika

Cook lobster tails as directed on package; drain. When cool enough to handle, cut through membranes lengthwise with kitchen shears. Remove membranes. Carefully remove lobster meat from shells; cube meat.

Heat oven to 350°. Prepare noodles Romanoff as directed on package except—use ⅔ cup milk. Stir in lobster, monosodium glutamate, and salt. Spoon mixture into shells. Pour remaining noodle mixture into oblong baking dish, 10x6x1½″, or into individual casseroles; place filled shells on top. Mix melted butter, lemon peel, and lemon juice; toss with artichoke hearts. Arrange artichokes on filled shells. Sprinkle with paprika. Cover dish tightly with aluminum foil. Bake 25 to 30 min. *4 servings.*

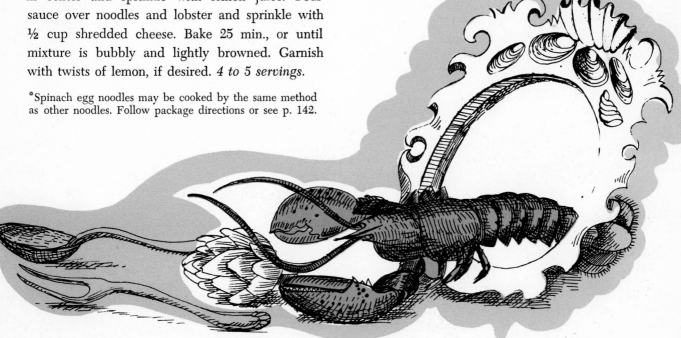

OYSTERS À LA CRÉMEUX

A creamy casserole of oysters, noodles, and cheese. Accompany with Best Tossed Salad (p. 149), a bowl of chilled grapes and apples for dessert.

2 cans (8 oz. each) oysters, drained (reserve liquor)
Milk
½ cup soft butter or margarine
1 egg
1 tbsp. flour
1 clove garlic, crushed
½ tsp. bottled brown bouquet sauce
¼ tsp. mace
Dash cayenne pepper

6 oz. noodles, cooked and drained
1¾ cups shredded process sharp American cheese
3 tbsp. minced parsley
¼ tsp. freshly ground black pepper
¼ cup shredded process sharp American cheese
¼ cup buttered bread crumbs

Heat oven to 350°. Add enough milk to reserved oyster liquor to make 2 cups. In a large heavy skillet, heat oysters and liquor 5 min. Mix butter, egg, flour, garlic, bouquet sauce, mace, and cayenne in a bowl. Stir slowly into oysters and liquor. Heat to boiling, stirring constantly. Boil 1 min. Stir in noodles, 1¾ cups cheese, parsley, and pepper. Pour into oblong baking dish, 11½x7½x1½". Sprinkle with ¼ cup cheese and bread crumbs. Bake uncovered 20 min., or until mixture is bubbly and lightly browned. *6 servings.*

PARTY TUNA BAKE

2 cans (7 oz. each) tuna, well drained
7 or 8 oz. noodles, cooked and drained
1½ cups dairy sour cream
¾ cup milk
1 can (3 oz.) sliced mushrooms, drained

1½ tsp. salt
¼ tsp. pepper
¼ cup fine dry bread crumbs
¼ cup grated Parmesan cheese
2 tbsp. butter or margarine, melted
Paprika

Heat oven to 350°. Stir together tuna, cooked noodles, sour cream, milk, mushrooms, salt, and pepper. Pour into 2-qt. casserole. Mix bread crumbs, Parmesan cheese, and melted butter; sprinkle over mixture in casserole. Sprinkle liberally with paprika. Bake uncovered 35 to 40 min., or until bubbly and hot. *6 to 8 servings.*

CHEESE-SHRIMP FONDUE

Fluffy as a soufflé, rich with cheese — an elegant dish for the bridge-group ladies!

10 slices white bread
6 eggs
3 cups milk
2 tbsp. minced parsley
¾ tsp. dry mustard

½ tsp. salt
2 cups shredded process sharp American cheese
2 cups cleaned cooked or canned shrimp

Heat oven to 325°. Remove crusts from bread; cut slices into cubes. Beat eggs, milk, and seasonings. Stir in bread cubes, cheese, and shrimp. Pour into oblong baking dish, 11½x7½x1½". Bake uncovered 1 hr., or until center is set. Serve immediately. *8 servings.*

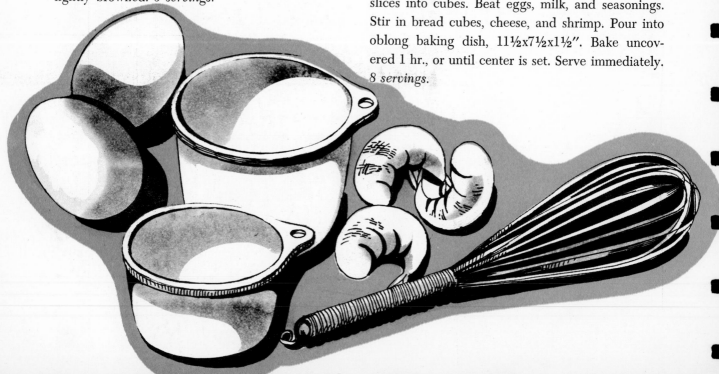

WAIKIKI PORK CHOP DINNER

7 or 8 oz. shell macaroni, cooked and drained	1 can (8 oz.) sliced mushrooms, drained
6 to 8 pork chops	6 to 8 pineapple slices
1 clove garlic	Curry Onion Sauce
Salt and pepper	(below)

Spread cooked macaroni in greased baking dish, 13x9½x2″, or 3-qt. casserole. Trim excess fat from chops; rub skillet with fat from one chop and with cut clove of garlic. Brown chops on both sides over medium heat. Season with salt and pepper. Cook and stir mushrooms in drippings about 5 min.

Heat oven to 350°. Sprinkle mushrooms over macaroni. Arrange chops on top of macaroni and top each with a slice of pineapple. Pour Curry Onion Sauce over chops and macaroni. Bake 1¼ to 1½ hr., or until chops are done. Garnish with parsley, if desired. *6 to 8 servings.*

CURRY ONION SAUCE

¼ cup butter or margarine	1 to 1½ tsp. curry
½ cup minced onion	powder
¼ cup Gold Medal Flour (regular or Wondra)	4 cups milk or chicken broth*
2 tsp. salt	

Melt butter in skillet used for chops. Add onion; cook and stir until tender. Remove from heat. Blend in flour, salt, and curry powder. Cook over low heat, stirring until mixture is bubbly. Remove from heat. Stir in milk. Heat to boiling, stirring constantly. Boil 1 min.

*Chicken broth may be made by dissolving 4 chicken bouillon cubes in 4 cups boiling water, or use canned chicken broth.

MAJESTIC STUFFED CHOPS

1 pkg. (10 oz.) frozen cranberry-orange relish, thawed	¼ tsp. pepper
	1 tbsp. shortening
4 thick loin pork chops (each with pocket for stuffing)	2 lb. rutabaga, pared and sliced into ½″ rounds
	Salt
2 tbsp. flour	¼ cup water
2 tsp. salt	Lettuce cups

Heat oven to 350°. Spoon 3 tbsp. cranberry-orange relish into each pocket of pork chops. Secure opening with wooden picks. Mix flour, 2 tsp. salt, and the pepper; rub meat with this mixture. Brown chops well in hot shortening. Arrange rutabaga rounds in the center of oblong baking dish, 13x 9½x2″. Sprinkle lightly with salt. Place chops beside rutabaga rounds. Pour water into skillet; stir and scrape the brown drippings loose from pan. Pour over chops and rutabaga. Cover with aluminum foil and bake 1½ hr., or until rutabaga is tender and chops are done—no pink in center. Serve remaining relish in lettuce cups. *4 servings.*

AUTUMN PORK CHOPS

6 pork chops, ½″ thick	¾ cup brown sugar
2 medium acorn squash	(packed)
¾ tsp. salt	¾ tsp. bottled brown
3 tbsp. butter or margarine	bouquet sauce
	2 to 4 tbsp. water

Heat oven to 350°. Trim excess fat from chops. Lightly grease hot skillet with fat from one chop; brown chops slowly on both sides. Pare squash, if desired. Slice into rings; remove seeds. Overlap squash and pork chops alternately in oblong baking dish, 11½x7½x1½″. Season with salt. Melt butter in skillet; blend in sugar and bouquet sauce. Stir in enough of the water to make a thin sauce; spoon over chops and squash. Cover; bake 1 hr., or until chops are done and squash is tender. During last 10 min. of baking, uncover and baste frequently with sauce. Add more water if needed. *6 servings.*

FRUITED HAM DINNER

A truly different and guest-worthy dinner in a baking dish; pictured below.

1 can (8 oz.) peach halves, undrained
1 can (8 oz.) pear halves, undrained
12 maraschino cherries, drained and halved
2 bananas, peeled and quartered
¼ tsp. pumpkin pie spice
2- to 3-lb. boneless fully cooked or canned ham*

4 to 6 medium sweet potatoes, cooked, peeled, and halved, or 1 can (1 lb. 11 oz.) sweet potatoes, drained
1 cup brown sugar (packed)
1 tsp. dry mustard

Combine fruits and pumpkin pie spice. Pour off and reserve ½ cup of the syrup. Heat oven to 350°. Place ham in oblong baking dish, 11½x7½x1½"; arrange sweet potato halves around ham. Mix brown sugar, reserved fruit syrup, and dry mustard. Pour over ham and potatoes. Bake uncovered 1 hr., basting ham and potatoes every 15 min. Drain spiced fruit and arrange attractively across top and around sides of ham. Bake uncovered 15 min. *4 to 6 servings.*

*Remove gelatin from canned ham before baking.

PARSLEY RICE-HAM SQUARES

Accompany this moist and tasty ham loaf with Cranberry Relish Mold (p. 150) and hot rolls.

1½ lb. ground ham
½ cup fine cracker crumbs
¾ cup milk
1 egg

Parsley Rice Filling (below)
Horseradish Sauce (below)

Heat oven to 350°. Mix ham, cracker crumbs, milk, and egg thoroughly. Spread half of mixture in square pan, 8x8x2". Spread Parsley Rice Filling over ham mixture. Top with remaining ham mixture. Bake 1 hr. Serve with Horseradish Sauce. *6 servings.*

PARSLEY RICE FILLING

Mix 1½ cups cooked rice with ⅓ cup minced parsley, 1 tbsp. butter or margarine, and dash pepper.

HORSERADISH SAUCE

2 tbsp. butter or margarine
2 tbsp. flour
1 cup chicken broth*
1 tbsp. drained prepared horseradish

1 tsp. prepared mustard
⅛ tsp. nutmeg
Salt to taste
Dash white pepper

Melt butter over low heat. Blend in flour. Cook over low heat, stirring until mixture is smooth and bubbly. Remove from heat. Stir in broth. Heat to boiling, stirring constantly. Boil 1 min. Stir in remaining ingredients. *Makes 1 cup.*

*Chicken broth may be made by dissolving 1 chicken bouillon cube in 1 cup boiling water, or use canned chicken broth.

CANADIAN BACON-ZUCCHINI BAKE

This out-of-the-ordinary, colorful dish can share the oven with a favorite baked dessert—perhaps pineapple upside-down cake, or gingerbread made from our mix.

2 lb. zucchini squash	1½ tsp. crushed marjoram
2 eggs	¾ tsp. salt
2 cups creamed cottage cheese	Few drops Tabasco
¾ cup uncooked instant rice	¾ cup grated Parmesan cheese
½ cup chopped onion	1 lb. Canadian bacon, cut into 16 slices
2 tbsp. minced parsley	

Heat oven to 350°. Cut unpared zucchini crosswise into ½″ slices. Cook covered in ½ to 1″ boiling salted water 5 min.; drain well. Beat eggs slightly with a fork; stir in remaining ingredients except Parmesan cheese and bacon. Arrange a layer of zucchini slices in oblong baking dish, 11½x7½x 1½″. Cover with half of cheese-rice mixture. Repeat layers, sprinkling top layer with Parmesan cheese. Overlap bacon slices on top. Bake uncovered 1 hr. *8 servings.*

GOURMET CASSEROLE

2 lb. bulk pork sausage	½ cup shredded process American cheese
½ cup chopped onion	
⅓ cup chopped green pepper	1 can (3 oz.) sliced mushrooms, undrained
1 can (10½ oz.) cream of mushroom soup	1 jar (2 oz.) sliced pimiento, drained
¾ cup milk	2 cups cooked wild rice
	2 cups cooked white rice

Heat oven to 350°. Shape sausage into 1½″ balls. Brown well on all sides; cover and cook 10 min. Remove sausage balls and drain on paper towels. Combine with remaining ingredients. Pour into 2-qt. casserole. Cover and bake 45 min., or until center is bubbly. Stir before serving. Garnish casserole with green pepper rings, if desired. *8 servings.*

BAKED HAM WITH SPINACH STUFFING

1 pkg. (10 oz.) frozen chopped spinach	¼ tsp. salt
	⅛ tsp. pepper
¼ cup diced celery	2 slices (½ lb. each) precooked ham, ¼ to ½″ thick
1 can (3 oz.) chopped mushrooms, drained	
2 tbsp. chopped onion	1 tbsp. butter, melted
2 tbsp. salad oil	Mustard Sauce (below)

Heat oven to 350°. Cook spinach as directed on package. Drain. Cook and stir celery, mushrooms, and onion in oil over medium heat until celery and onion are tender. Add to spinach. Stir in salt and pepper. Place one ham slice in a shallow baking dish. Spread with spinach mixture. Top with remaining ham slice. Brush with melted butter. Cover and bake 15 min. Uncover and continue baking about 15 min., or until lightly browned. Serve with Mustard Sauce. *4 to 6 servings.*

MUSTARD SAUCE

2 tbsp. butter or margarine	1 tbsp. well-drained prepared horseradish
2 tbsp. flour	
1¼ cups milk	1 tbsp. prepared mustard
⅛ tsp. nutmeg	Salt and pepper to taste

Melt butter over low heat in heavy saucepan. Blend in flour, Cook over low heat, stirring until mixture is smooth and bubbly. Remove from heat. Stir in milk. Heat to boiling, stirring constantly. Boil 1 min. Blend in seasonings.

GROUND BEEF AU VIN

¼ cup finely chopped
  onion
2 tbsp. butter or margarine
1 lb. ground beef
¼ cup soft bread crumbs
1 small clove garlic,
  minced
1 egg
1 tsp. salt
¼ tsp. pepper
¼ tsp. crushed oregano

5 slices bacon
½ lb. fresh mushrooms,
  sliced, or 1 can (3 oz.)
  sliced mushrooms,
  drained
1 tbsp. butter or margarine
1 can (10½ oz.) cream of
  mushroom soup
½ cup red Burgundy
3 to 4 cups hot cooked rice

Heat oven to 350°. Cook onion in 2 tbsp. butter until tender. Lift onion with slotted spoon and add to the ground beef in a large mixing bowl. Brown bread crumbs and garlic in same skillet; add to ground beef mixture. Add egg and seasonings. Mix until blended; shape into 1″ balls. Fry bacon until crisp; drain on paper towels. Brown meatballs in small amount of bacon fat and place in 1½-qt. casserole. Cook and stir mushrooms in 1 tbsp. butter. Blend in soup and Burgundy. Pour over meatballs. Crumble bacon over top. Cover; bake 45 min. Serve with rice. *4 to 6 servings.*

HARVEST MEDLEY

This colorful casserole is pictured below.

1 lb. ground beef
½ lb. ground pork
½ cup minced onion
¾ cup dry bread crumbs
1 tbsp. minced parsley
1½ tsp. salt
¼ tsp. crushed basil
⅛ tsp. pepper
1 tsp. Worcestershire
  sauce
1 egg
½ cup milk
⅓ cup butter

1 medium onion, sliced
1 green pepper, cut into
  ½″ pieces
½ medium eggplant,
  pared and cubed
1 lb. Hubbard or acorn
  squash, pared and
  cubed
4 tomatoes, peeled and
  cut into eighths
¼ cup shredded
  Cheddar cheese
¼ cup bread crumbs

Heat oven to 350°. Mix meat, minced onion, ¾ cup crumbs, next 5 seasonings, egg, and milk; shape into 1″ balls. Brown in butter; remove. Cook and stir onion in butter until tender; season lightly with salt and pepper. Remove from skillet. Repeat with next 3 vegetables, cooking each separately. (For squash, add small amount water; cover until tender.) Lightly mix vegetables, meatballs, and tomatoes; place in 2-qt. casserole. Top with cheese and crumbs. Bake 20 to 25 min. *6 servings.*

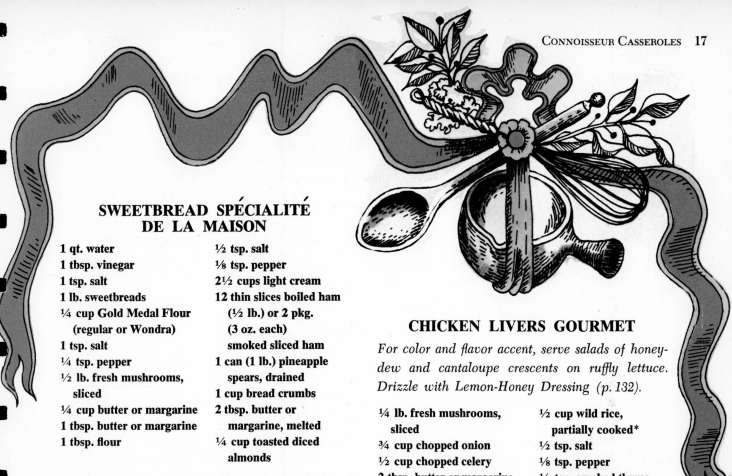

SWEETBREAD SPÉCIALITÉ DE LA MAISON

1 qt. water
1 tbsp. vinegar
1 tsp. salt
1 lb. sweetbreads
¼ cup Gold Medal Flour
    (regular or Wondra)
1 tsp. salt
¼ tsp. pepper
½ lb. fresh mushrooms,
    sliced
¼ cup butter or margarine
1 tbsp. butter or margarine
1 tbsp. flour

½ tsp. salt
⅛ tsp. pepper
2½ cups light cream
12 thin slices boiled ham
    (½ lb.) or 2 pkg.
    (3 oz. each)
    smoked sliced ham
1 can (1 lb.) pineapple
    spears, drained
1 cup bread crumbs
2 tbsp. butter or
    margarine, melted
¼ cup toasted diced
    almonds

Combine water, vinegar, and 1 tsp. salt; bring to boiling. Add sweetbreads and simmer 30 min. Drain; rinse well in cold water. Remove membranes; cut into 1″ pieces.

Heat oven to 350°. Mix ¼ cup flour, 1 tsp. salt, and ¼ tsp. pepper; coat sweetbreads with flour mixture. Brown sweetbreads and mushrooms in ¼ cup butter. Remove to oblong baking dish, 11½x7½x1½″. Melt 1 tbsp. butter in skillet; blend in 1 tbsp. flour, ½ tsp. salt, and ⅛ tsp. pepper. Cook over low heat, stirring until mixture is smooth and bubbly. Remove from heat. Stir in cream. Heat to boiling, stirring constantly. Boil 1 min. Pour over sweetbreads and mushrooms in baking dish. Wrap each slice of ham around a pineapple spear; arrange on top of sweetbread mixture. Toss bread crumbs with melted butter. Sprinkle buttered crumbs and almonds over top of ham rolls. Bake 25 to 30 min. Garnish with remaining pineapple spears and parsley, if desired. *6 servings.*

CHICKEN LIVERS GOURMET

For color and flavor accent, serve salads of honeydew and cantaloupe crescents on ruffly lettuce. Drizzle with Lemon-Honey Dressing (p. 132).

¼ lb. fresh mushrooms,
    sliced
¾ cup chopped onion
½ cup chopped celery
2 tbsp. butter or margarine
2 cans (13¾ oz. each)
    chicken broth
½ cup uncooked regular
    rice

½ cup wild rice,
    partially cooked*
½ tsp. salt
⅛ tsp. pepper
¼ tsp. crushed thyme
4 slices bacon
1 lb. chicken livers
¼ cup Gold Medal Flour
    (regular or Wondra)
¼ cup minced parsley

Heat oven to 350°. Cook and stir mushrooms, onion, and celery in butter until tender. Stir in chicken broth and heat to boiling. Place rice, salt, pepper, and thyme in 2-qt. casserole. Pour chicken broth mixture over rice and seasonings; stir to mix. Cover and bake 30 min. Fry bacon and drain on paper towels. Coat chicken livers with flour; brown on all sides in bacon drippings. Remove casserole from oven and stir in minced parsley. Arrange chicken livers around edge of dish. Cover and bake 30 min. longer, or until rice is cooked. Before serving, crumble bacon; sprinkle in center of casserole. Garnish with additional parsley. *4 to 6 servings.*

*Pour 2 cups boiling water over uncooked wild rice. Cover; let stand 20 min. Drain.

CONNOISSEUR CASSEROLES —ON THE DOUBLE

CURRIED SHRIMP BAKE

For those spur-of-the-moment parties.

1 can (10 oz.) frozen cream of shrimp soup	4 oz. elbow macaroni, cooked and drained
¾ cup milk	2 cups cleaned cooked or canned shrimp
2 tbsp. minced parsley	Buttered bread crumbs
½ tsp. salt	
½ to 1 tsp. curry powder	

Heat oven to 375°. Heat soup, milk, parsley, salt, and curry powder in saucepan; stir constantly. Stir macaroni and shrimp into soup mixture. Pour into buttered 1½-qt. casserole. Top with buttered bread crumbs. Bake 30 min., or until bubbly. *4 servings.*

ALMONDINE DE LA MER

A gourmet tuna-noodle casserole.

1 pkg. of our noodles almondine	1 can (6½ oz.) tuna, drained
2 cups boiling water	2 tbsp. chopped pimiento
1 can (8½ oz.) peas, drained	2 tbsp. chopped onion

Heat oven to 375°. Empty noodles into 2-qt. casserole. Sprinkle with packet of seasoned sauce mix. Stir in remaining ingredients. Cover; bake 20 to 25 min. Remove from oven; stir mixture slightly. Sprinkle packet of almonds over top before serving. *4 servings.*

STROGANOFF CASSEROLE

2 lb. ground beef	2 cans (10½ oz. each) cream of mushroom soup
2 tbsp. shortening	
2 qt. water (8 cups)	
2 tsp. salt	2 tbsp. instant minced onion
2 pkg. of our noodles Romanoff	
	2 tbsp. chopped pimiento
2 cups milk	½ cup crushed Wheaties
¼ cup butter or margarine	

Heat oven to 350°. Brown ground beef in hot fat; drain. In 4-qt. saucepan, heat water to boiling; add salt and noodles. Boil 7 to 8 min., or until tender, stirring occasionally. Drain noodles thoroughly. (Do not rinse.) Blend in sour cream-cheese sauce mix, milk, and butter. Stir in meat, soup, onion, and pimiento. Pour into 3-qt. casserole. Bake uncovered 25 min. Sprinkle Wheaties over top. Bake 5 min. longer, or until crumbs are toasted. Garnish with parsley, if desired. *10 to 12 servings.*

NOODLES VAL D'ISÈRE

A hidden layer of sour cream and cheese.

½ lb. ground beef	1⅓ cups hot water
½ tsp. salt	1 pkg. (3 oz.) cream cheese, softened
1 pkg. of our noodles Italiano	¼ cup dairy sour cream
	1 tbsp. minced parsley

Heat oven to 375°. Brown ground beef with salt. Cook and drain noodles as directed on package. Return to saucepan; blend in packet of tomato sauce mix and water. Blend cream cheese, sour cream, parsley, and the packet of cheese mix until smooth and creamy. In 1½-qt. casserole, layer half of noodles and sauce, the ground beef, and cheese mixture. Top with remaining noodles and sauce. Bake uncovered 20 to 25 min. *4 servings.*

Duet Dishes

Among the most interesting and popular of party foods are those two-part harmonies of texture and taste we call our Duet Dishes. Part one, the rich and artfully seasoned food in a sauce, may be cooked to perfection in your choice of skillet, chafing dish, or saucepan. Part two, the fluffy rice or tender pasta or the crisp toast cups or pastry shells which form the base for the dish, is simple to prepare following our "Kitchen-tested" directions on page 29 and pages 140-142.

Best of all, Duet Dishes are versatile triumphs of good taste whenever you serve them—at luncheon, dinner, or midnight supper.

DINNER IN A CHAFING DISH

For drama at the dinner table, cooking à la chafing dish in the presence of your guests is unsurpassed! Plan to do this only for a small party, however, since most chafing dishes are limited to 2-quart capacity. You will find it surprisingly easy, festive and fun to do, but rarely speedy. So, if you must hurry, take the shortcut many clever hostesses do and finish all basic cooking on the range top—in a skillet or right in the blazer pan. Then garnish and serve glamorously from the chafing dish at the table, where food will keep appetizingly hot for second servings.

THE CHAFING DISH—Types and parts.

• This famous pan ensemble is really "kissin' cousin" to the familiar double boiler and a member of a large and distinguished family of cooking dishes that are complete with their own sources of heat. Its relatives are the single pan skillet without water pan, the crêpes suzette pan, electric skillet, and the continental earthenware fondue dish with rounded bowl-shaped bottom. Best for your purposes probably will be a chafing dish with a blazer pan (often tin lined), a water pan, burner, and stand. Choose from modern or traditional design—copper, silver, stainless, or aluminum.

THE FLAME—From alcohol or canned heat?

• Chafing dishes burn either liquid alcohol or canned heat (solidified alcohol). Your choice will depend on the kind and amount of actual cooking you plan to do in it. An alcohol burner gives a hotter flame than canned heat, is more easily controlled, and uses less-expensive fuel. However, it consumes fuel quickly and refilling the burner during cooking can be awkward and inconvenient. Some alcohol burners have a wick; these give somewhat less heat and are usually more difficult to regulate. Canned heat is easy to handle and adequate for cooking that does not require a high, intense flame. For all types, check the heat control when you buy to be sure it is easy to regulate.

ACCESSORIES—Handy and attractive.

• In addition to the chafing dish with a tray beneath it, you will need a wooden spoon to avoid scratching the dish, salt and pepper shakers, sometimes a wire whisk. A second tray will hold all necessary utensils and pre-measured ingredients.

BASIC PREPARATION—Behind the scene.

• Beforehand, cut or chop ingredients into uniform, attractive pieces and measure the seasonings exactly. Assemble in small dishes on the tray and carry to the table. Keep the water pan filled with boiling water to a depth of about two inches, never allowing it to touch the blazer pan above.

CHICKEN OR TURKEY À LA KING

A reliable company favorite.

**1 can (6 oz.) sliced
  mushrooms, drained**
½ cup diced green pepper
½ cup butter or margarine
**½ cup Gold Medal Flour
  (regular or Wondra)**
1 tsp. salt
¼ tsp. pepper

2 cups chicken broth*
2 cups light cream
**2 cups cubed cooked
  chicken or turkey**
**1 jar (4 oz.) pimiento,
  chopped**
**Patty Shells, Tart Shells,
  or Toast Cups (p. 29)**

Cook and stir mushrooms and green pepper in butter 5 min. Remove from heat. Blend in flour, salt, and pepper. Cook over low heat, stirring until mixture is bubbly. Remove from heat. Stir in broth and cream. Heat to boiling, stirring constantly. Boil 1 min. Add chicken and pimiento; heat through. Serve hot in Patty Shells, Tart Shells, or Toast Cups. *8 servings.*

*Chicken broth may be made by dissolving 2 chicken bouillon cubes in 2 cups boiling water, or use canned chicken broth.

SMOKED TURKEY ROYALE

Rich, creamy sauce brimming with pieces of smoked turkey and bright green broccoli. Accent the meal with Cranberry Relish Mold (p. 150).

¼ cup butter or margarine
**¼ cup Gold Medal Flour
  (regular or Wondra)**
¼ tsp. pepper
¼ tsp. sage
¾ cup light cream
**1 can (13¾ oz.) chicken
  broth**

**1 pkg. (10 oz.) frozen
  chopped broccoli,
  cooked and drained**
**2 pkg. (3 oz. each) sliced
  smoked turkey, cut up**
**½ cup shredded Cheddar
  cheese**
**Tart Shells (p. 29) or
  3 cups hot cooked rice**

Melt butter over low heat in heavy saucepan, skillet, or blazer pan of chafing dish. Blend in flour, pepper, and sage. Cook over low heat, stirring until mixture is smooth and bubbly. Remove from heat. Blend in cream and broth. Heat to boiling, stirring constantly. Boil 1 min. Stir in broccoli and turkey; heat through. Sprinkle with cheese. Cover and let stand until cheese is melted. Serve in Tart Shells or over rice. *6 servings.*

ONE-STEP CREAM SAUCE
When using Gold Medal Wondra Flour in your cream sauce, thoroughly blend the Wondra and seasonings into <u>cold</u> liquid. Add butter and heat to boiling over medium heat, stirring constantly. Boil 1 min.

SHRIMP CREOLE

Start this New Orleans-style dinner, pictured here, with onion soup. Your salad? A crisp green one of romaine tossed with marinated artichoke hearts and Classic French Dressing (p. 149). Choose Pecan Pie or Crème Brûlée for dessert.

1½ cups chopped onion	1 cup water
1 cup finely chopped celery	2 tsp. minced parsley
2 medium green peppers, finely chopped	1 tsp. salt
2 cloves garlic, minced	⅛ tsp. cayenne pepper
¼ cup butter or margarine	2 bay leaves, crushed
1 can (15 oz.) tomato sauce	14 to 16 oz. cleaned raw shrimp, fresh or frozen*
	3 cups hot cooked rice

Cook and stir onion, celery, green pepper, and garlic in butter about 5 min., or until tender. Remove from heat; stir in tomato sauce, water, and seasonings. Simmer 10 min. Add additional water, if needed. Add shrimp. Heat mixture to boiling; cover and cook over medium heat 10 to 20 min., or until shrimp are pink and tender. Serve over hot cooked rice. *6 servings.*

*Run frozen shrimp under cold water to remove ice glaze before adding shrimp to sauce.

SHRIMP ÉLÉGANTE IN TART SHELLS

A rich, elegant dish. Serve with fresh spinach salad, strawberry sundaes for dessert.

1½ cups milk	⅛ tsp. pepper
3 tbsp. coarsely chopped onion	1 cup cooked green peas
4 sprigs parsley	1 cup cleaned cooked or canned shrimp
1 clove garlic, peeled	2 egg yolks, slightly beaten
1 bay leaf, crumbled	
3 tbsp. butter or margarine	2 tsp. lemon juice
3 tbsp. flour	Tart Shells (p. 29)
½ tsp. salt	Lemon wedges

Heat milk with onion, parsley, garlic, and bay leaf to scalding; strain. Melt butter in skillet, saucepan, or blazer pan of chafing dish; blend in flour, salt, and pepper. Cook over low heat, stirring until mixture is smooth and bubbly. Remove from heat. Stir in hot milk. Heat to boiling, stirring constantly. Boil 1 min. Add peas and shrimp; heat through. Stir a little of the hot mixture into egg yolks. Mix into remaining hot mixture. Stir in lemon juice. Cook 1 min. longer. Serve hot in warm Tart Shells. Pass lemon wedges. *4 servings.*

Betty Crocker Note: To release flavor, slash garlic clove several times with sharp knife.

CHICKEN AND CRAB VALENTINE

3 tbsp. butter or margarine
3 tbsp. flour
½ tsp. salt
½ tsp. paprika
⅛ tsp. nutmeg
1 cup chicken broth*
1 cup dairy sour cream
5 or 6 drops Tabasco
⅛ tsp. garlic powder
1½ cups diced cooked
    chicken

1 can (7¾ oz.) crabmeat,
    drained and cartilage
    removed
4 slices cooked bacon,
    crumbled
1 pkg. (10 oz.) frozen
    green peas, cooked
    and drained
Toast Points (p. 29)

Melt butter in skillet, saucepan, or blazer pan of chafing dish. Blend in flour and seasonings. Cook over low heat, stirring until mixture is smooth and bubbly. Remove from heat. Stir in chicken broth. Heat to boiling, stirring constantly. Boil 1 min. Remove from heat. Slowly stir in sour cream, Tabasco, and garlic powder. Add chicken, crabmeat, and ¾ of the crumbled bacon. Heat through, stirring constantly. Pour mixture into serving dish or serve over water bath of chafing dish. Arrange hot cooked peas around edge of dish. Mound remaining crumbled bacon in center. Serve over Toast Points. *4 to 6 servings.*

*Chicken broth may be made by dissolving 1 chicken bouillon cube in 1 cup boiling water, or use canned chicken broth.

CRAB NEWPORT IN SHELL RING

7 to 8 oz. shell macaroni,
    cooked and drained
1 cup finely shredded
    Cheddar cheese

Creamed Crabmeat and
    Mushroom Sauce
    (below)
¼ cup buttered bread
    crumbs
Minced parsley

Lightly toss hot macaroni with cheese until all cheese is melted. Spoon a ring of macaroni-cheese mixture on serving plate. Fill center with Creamed Crabmeat and Mushroom Sauce. Sprinkle crumbs in a ring around outer edge of sauce; circle with parsley. *6 servings.*

CREAMED CRABMEAT AND MUSHROOM SAUCE

1 can (6 oz.) sliced
    mushrooms, drained
    (reserve liquid)
1 tbsp. minced onion
1 tbsp. chopped chives
1 tbsp. minced parsley
¼ cup butter or margarine
2 tbsp. flour
1 tsp. salt
Dash cayenne pepper
Dash nutmeg

¾ cup liquid (mushroom
    liquid and water)
2 egg yolks, slightly
    beaten
1½ cups dairy sour
    cream
1 can (5 to 7 oz.) crab-
    meat, lobster, or
    minced clams,
    drained
2 tbsp. sherry

Cook and stir mushrooms, onion, chives, and parsley in butter over low heat for 5 min. Remove from heat. Blend in flour, salt, cayenne pepper, and nutmeg. Cook over low heat, stirring until mixture is bubbly. Remove from heat. Stir in the liquid. Heat to boiling, stirring constantly. Boil 1 min. Remove from heat. Blend egg yolks and sour cream; stir into hot mixture with the crabmeat and sherry. Heat through, stirring constantly.

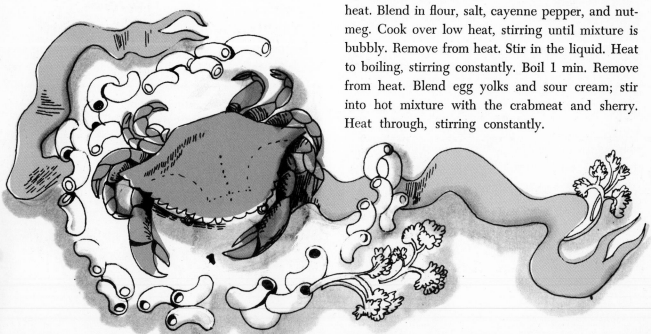

CURRIED HADDOCK
IN POLKA-DOT RING

Pictured above.

1 lb. haddock fillets
¼ tsp. salt
½ cup boiling water
¼ cup minced onion
2 tbsp. butter or margarine
2 tbsp. flour
1 tsp. curry powder
1 tsp. sugar

¼ tsp. salt
Dash ginger
¾ cup milk
3 cups hot cooked rice
1 pkg. (10 oz.) frozen green peas, cooked and drained

In tightly covered saucepan, simmer fillets in ¼ tsp. salt and boiling water for 6 to 10 min., or until easily broken apart with fork. Drain, reserving broth. Break fillets into 2″ pieces.

Cook and stir onion in butter until tender. Remove from heat. Blend in flour and seasonings. Cook over low heat, stirring until mixture is bubbly. Remove from heat. Stir in ½ cup reserved fish broth and the milk. Heat to boiling, stirring constantly. Boil 1 min. Stir in fish; heat through.

Mix rice and hot peas; pack lightly in greased 9″ ring mold. Unmold on large serving dish; pour curry into center of mold. *4 to 6 servings.*

PARTY SEAFOOD

⅓ cup finely chopped onion
1 medium green pepper, finely chopped
1 can (3 oz.) sliced mushrooms, drained
¼ cup butter or margarine
⅓ cup Gold Medal Flour (regular or Wondra)
1 tsp. salt
¼ tsp. pepper
2 cups milk

¾ cup shredded process sharp American cheese
1 tbsp. lemon juice
½ tsp. dry mustard
¼ tsp. Worcestershire sauce
1 can (7¾ oz.) crabmeat, drained and cartilage removed
1 cup cleaned cooked or canned shrimp
Tart Shells or Toast Cups (p. 29)

Cook and stir onion, green pepper, and mushrooms in butter until onion is tender. Remove from heat. Blend in flour and seasonings. Cook over low heat, stirring until the mixture is hot. Remove from heat. Stir in 1 cup of the milk. Heat to boiling, stirring constantly. Boil 1 min. Stir in remaining 1 cup milk, the cheese, lemon juice, dry mustard, and Worcestershire sauce; stir until cheese is melted. Mix in crabmeat and shrimp; heat through. Serve in Tart Shells or Toast Cups. *4 to 6 servings.*

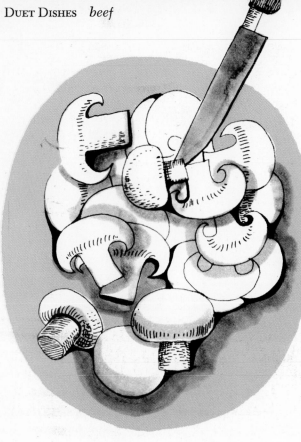

CLASSIC BEEF STROGANOFF

1 lb. beef sirloin steak or tenderloin	2 tbsp. catsup
½ lb. fresh mushrooms, sliced	1 small clove garlic, minced
½ cup minced onion	1 tsp. salt
2 tbsp. butter or margarine	3 tbsp. flour
1 can (10½ oz.) beef consommé	1 cup dairy sour cream
	3 to 4 cups hot cooked noodles or rice

Cut meat diagonally into very thin slices. Cook and stir mushrooms and onion in butter until onion is tender; remove from skillet. In same skillet, brown meat lightly on both sides. Set aside ⅓ cup consommé; stir remaining consommé, the catsup, garlic, and salt into skillet. Cover and simmer 15 min. Blend reserved ⅓ cup consommé and flour; stir into skillet. Add mushrooms and onion. Heat to boiling, stirring constantly. Boil 1 min. Stir in sour cream; heat through. Serve over hot noodles or rice. *4 servings.*

SUCCOTASH SUPPER

Great for guests on Sunday night, or for a midnight supper.

1 lb. ground beef	1 tbsp. shortening
3 tbsp. flour	1 pkg. (10 oz.) frozen succotash, cooked and drained
¼ tsp. garlic powder	
¼ tsp. celery seed	
Dash cayenne pepper	3 cups chow mein noodles
½ cup water	
2 tbsp. soy sauce	Mushroom Sauce (below)

Mix ground beef, flour, garlic powder, celery seed, cayenne pepper, water, and soy sauce. Melt shortening in skillet or blazer pan of chafing dish; add meat mixture and cook, stirring constantly, until meat is no longer pink. Add succotash and continue to cook, stirring constantly, until heated through. Serve mixture over crisp, warm chow mein noodles. Pour Mushroom Sauce over top. *4 to 6 servings.*

MUSHROOM SAUCE

In heavy saucepan, slowly stir ¼ cup light cream or milk into 1 can (10½ oz.) cream of mushroom soup. Cook and stir over low heat until hot.

HUNGARIAN GOULASH

2 lb. beef chuck or bottom round, cut into 1″ cubes	2 tsp. paprika
	2 tsp. salt
	½ tsp. dry mustard
¼ cup shortening	Dash red pepper
1 cup sliced onion	1½ cups water
1 small clove garlic, minced	2 tbsp. flour
¾ cup catsup	¼ cup cold water
1 tbsp. brown sugar	7 or 8 oz. noodles, cooked and drained
2 tbsp. Worcestershire sauce	

Brown beef in hot shortening. Add onion and garlic; cook and stir until onion is tender. Mix catsup and seasonings; add to skillet and stir to mix. Add 1½ cups water; cover and simmer 2 to 2½ hr. Blend flour and ¼ cup cold water; stir into meat mixture. Heat to boiling, stirring constantly. Boil 1 min. Pour over hot cooked noodles. Garnish with parsley, if desired. *6 to 8 servings.*

BEEF AND ASPARAGUS SAVORY

So colorful and tasty you know it's just right for a spring or summertime meal.

1 pkg. (10 oz.) frozen asparagus cuts or 1 lb. fresh asparagus, cut up	1 tbsp. flour
	⅔ cup milk
	½ cup shredded Cheddar cheese
2 tbsp. finely chopped onion	2 tbsp. chopped pimiento
4 oz. dried beef, shredded	Toast Cups (p. 29) or
3 tbsp. butter or margarine	Quick Corn Bread (p. 152)

Cook asparagus in boiling salted water until just tender, 8 to 10 min. Drain. Cook and stir onion and dried beef in butter until onion is tender. Remove from heat. Blend in flour. Cook over low heat, stirring until mixture is bubbly. Remove from heat. Stir in milk. Heat to boiling, stirring constantly. Boil 1 min. Stir in cheese, asparagus, and pimiento; heat through. Serve in Toast Cups or over split squares of Corn Bread. *4 to 6 servings.*

Betty Crocker Note: If dried beef is very salty, pour boiling water over it and drain well before using.

CALIFORNIA "CHIPPED" BEEF

Creamed dried beef with an avocado plus! Bright red tomatoes garnish the plate and double as salad. Pictured below.

4 oz. dried beef, cut up	2 cups light cream or milk
¼ cup butter or margarine	1 hard-cooked egg, chopped
¼ cup Gold Medal Flour (regular or Wondra)	1 ripe avocado, peeled and diced
¼ tsp. nutmeg	Poppy Seed Cups (p. 29)
¼ tsp. pepper	Tomato wedges
Dash cayenne pepper	

In saucepan, skillet, or blazer pan of chafing dish, cook and stir dried beef in butter until edges curl. Remove from heat. Blend in flour and seasonings. Cook over low heat, stirring until mixture is hot. Remove from heat. Stir in cream. Heat to boiling, stirring constantly. Boil 1 min. Gently stir in egg and avocado; heat through. Serve in Poppy Seed Cups. Arrange on plates with tomato wedges. Trim plate with hard-cooked egg wedges and olives, if desired. *6 servings.*

IT'S A PARTY WITH FONDUE!

Bread and cheese . . . simple, yet so exciting to eat when the cheese is melted and the bread dunked. Known as cheese fondue, this Swiss ceremonial specialty is cooked and served at the table in a special colored earthenware dish over its own flame. A chafing dish or electric skillet may be substituted, but remember to keep the heat so low that the cheese barely bubbles.

Fondue must be stirred constantly by one guest at a time, who spears a chunk of crusty French bread with his long-handled fondue fork, dips, stirs, and twirls the cheese around the bread to eat it. Custom decrees that whoever loses his bread in the fondue pays the penalty of a kiss or plays host to the next fondue party.

CHEESE FONDUE CONTINENTAL

This simple variation of the traditional Swiss fondue is pictured here.

8 oz. sharp natural
   Cheddar cheese,
   shredded
1 pkg. (8 oz.) natural
   Swiss cheese, shredded*
2 tbsp. flour
½ tsp. salt

¼ tsp. pepper
1 clove garlic
1 can (12 oz.) beer
Dash Tabasco
French bread, cut into
   1″ cubes

Mix cheeses, flour, salt, and pepper in large bowl. Rub cut clove of garlic around bottom and sides of an earthenware fondue casserole, blazer pan of chafing dish, or heavy skillet. Pour in beer and heat slowly; *gradually* stir in cheese mixture, adding only a cup at a time and stirring after each addition until cheese is melted and blended. (Do not allow mixture to become too hot.) Stir in Tabasco. Serve immediately over very low heat, stirring constantly. (If fondue becomes too thick, stir in a little additional heated beer.) To eat fondue, spear cube of bread with long-handled fork and dip into the cheese. *4 servings.*

*The Swiss cheese should be aged 6 months.

MOCK CHEESE FONDUE

1 can (11 oz.) Cheddar
   cheese soup (undiluted)
1 clove garlic, minced
2 egg yolks, beaten

¼ cup apple cider or
   juice
French bread, cut into
   1″ cubes

In saucepan or blazer pan of chafing dish, heat soup and garlic to just below boiling; remove from heat. Stir half of the hot soup into beaten egg yolks; blend the mixture into remaining soup. Stir in cider. Heat through, stirring constantly. Keep warm over low heat. To eat fondue, spear cube of bread with long-handled fork and dip into cheese. *4 servings.*

DUET DISHES— ON THE DOUBLE

NOODLE RING WITH CRABMEAT ROMANOFF

1 pkg. of our noodles
 Romanoff
¼ cup milk

¼ cup minced parsley,
 if desired
Crabmeat Romanoff
 (below)

Heat oven to 350°. Cook and drain noodles as directed on package. Blend in ¼ cup of the sour cream-cheese sauce mix and milk. Stir in parsley. Lightly pack into well-buttered 1-qt. ring mold. Set in pan of water (1″ deep). Bake 15 min. Unmold; fill center with Crabmeat Romanoff. Garnish with parsley, if desired. *4 to 6 servings.*

CRABMEAT ROMANOFF

Drain 1 can (3 oz.) sliced mushrooms. Cook and stir mushrooms in 2 tbsp. butter 2 min. Remove from heat. Add ⅔ cup milk. Heat to boiling. Stir in the remaining sour cream-cheese sauce mix until smooth. Drain 1 can (6½ oz.) crabmeat and remove cartilage; stir crabmeat into sauce. Heat through. Pour into center of noodle ring.

SPEEDY CHICKEN-SHRIMP CURRY

1 medium onion, diced
1 medium apple, pared
 and diced
3 to 4 tbsp. butter or
 margarine
2 cans (10½ oz. each)
 chicken à la king

1 can (4½ oz.) deveined
 shrimp, drained
2 tbsp. lemon juice
2 to 3 tsp. curry powder
3 cups hot cooked rice
Curry accompaniments

Cook and stir onion and apple in butter 2 to 3 min. Add chicken à la king, shrimp, lemon juice, and curry powder; heat through. Serve over hot cooked rice with side dishes of curry accompaniments such as coconut, chutney, raisins, slivered almonds, chopped salted peanuts, crisp bacon bits, India relish, chopped hard-cooked eggs, and preserved kumquats. *4 to 6 servings.*

"SERVE-WITHS" FOR DUET DISHES

TART SHELLS

1½ cups Gold Medal Flour (regular or Wondra)	½ cup plus 2 tbsp. shortening
¾ tsp. salt	3 tbsp. water

Heat oven to 475°. Mix flour and salt. Cut in shortening thoroughly. Sprinkle water gradually over mixture, a tbsp. at a time, tossing lightly with a fork after each addition.* (If dough is dry, a few drops of water may be added.) Gather dough into 8 equal balls. On lightly floured cloth-covered board, roll each ball into 4″ circle. Fit circles into tart pans. *Or* fit pastry circles over backs of muffin cups or custard cups, making pleats so pastry will fit closely. Prick with fork to prevent puffing during baking. Place cups on baking sheet. Bake 8 to 10 min. When cool, remove from pans. *Makes 8 tart shells.*

*Doughs made with Gold Medal Wondra may look and feel different. Work dough until it holds together.

SPEEDY TART SHELLS

Prepare pastry for One-crust Pie as directed on inside wrapper of our pie crust mix. Divide dough into 6 to 8 parts. Roll out and bake as directed in Tart Shells (above).

TOAST CUPS

Heat oven to 375°. Trim crusts from thinly sliced fresh bread; spread with soft butter. Press buttered side down into muffin cups. Bake 12 min., or until lightly toasted.

POPPY SEED CUPS

Make Toast Cups (above) except—sprinkle buttered side with poppy seed before pressing into muffin cups.

TOAST POINTS

Remove crusts from slices of bread; toast. Cut each slice into 4 triangles.

PATTY SHELLS

For fast and easy-to-fix patty shells, use packaged frozen ones. Just follow package directions for baking.

Crowd-size Suppers

From the "covered-dish suppers" of horse-and-carriage days to the potluck dinners of the modern PTA, sharing food has been a common denominator of groups which work or celebrate together. "Will everybody like it?" and "Can we afford to serve it?" are questions every hostess and food-committee chairman must answer.

Whether you're serving in your own home or in a church dining room, you will find these recipes, planned for 24, answer your needs for popular, economical, and even exciting "quantity" meals.

THE QUANTITY QUANDARY

Serving dinner to more than 10 guests? Then you're cooking in quantity! How to plan, what to serve, and how much to buy can be a problem to any homemaker confronted with this task. The occasion may be a potluck supper, club meeting, church or school function, or the latest community fund-raising venture . . . and you're in charge! Be assured with a recipe from this chapter and with these step-by-step pointers.

ORGANIZATION—The key to smooth success.

• When cooking for a crowd is a group project, appoint a general chairman (unless you're already it). With one capable person in charge, conflicting opinions and confusion are avoided.

• Set up committees—one each for planning, food preparation, serving, and cleanup. The planning committee usually includes the chairman and heads of committees.

THE RECIPES AND MENU—Suited to your guests.

• First choose any of the easy-to-do recipes from this chapter, then plan the menu around it. Each recipe will serve 24. If more servings are needed, you will find it easier to repeat the recipe as given rather than to mix and cook a doubled or tripled recipe all at once—unless, of course, you have access to restaurant equipment.

• Choose recipes and a menu that will appeal to those being served; think of their ages, tastes, and appetites. Be sure to suit the menu to the equipment and help available. And do plan an exciting and interesting menu. Include a seasonal food or two for fresh flavor accent—a few red strawberries or sliced tomatoes as a garnish on each plate add greatly to appetite appeal.

• Compile a marketing list after you have selected all the recipes. To estimate the number to be fed, count reservations and add the number of workers (they must eat, too). Once you know how many to expect, determine the amount of each recipe needed and complete an order list.

THE FOOD—Prepared according to plan.

• List extra cooking utensils you'll need. Make arrangements to buy or borrow them.

• Supply each cook with her own copy of menu, recipes, and work schedule.

• Cook as much as possible the day before. For instance, if you're preparing hot breads, mix the dry ingredients ahead of time. Prepare salad dressings, refrigerated gelatin salads, and desserts.

• If your home, school, or church kitchen is too small for many cooks, some hot dishes may be prepared and refrigerated by committee members in their own kitchens. In this case, there must be adequate facilities for on-the-spot reheating.

• Food preparation and storage must include proper safeguards for the health of the people you feed. Cleanliness of all equipment, ingredients, and persons handling the food is essential. Do not allow food to stand at room temperature but keep it hot, or well chilled in the refrigerator.

SUPPLIES AND SERVICE—Systemized for efficiency.

• The serving committee checks on table linen, silver, china, glassware, and other table accessories. Mix-match china, if necessary, to acquire enough for serving. Just alternate the patterns at each place, and your tables will look attractive and orderly. If you borrow dishes, identify each on the underside with nail polish which can be removed later with polish remover.

• Have all tables set beforehand. Place bread, butter, glasses of iced water on table just before guests are seated.

• Depending on space and facilities available, serve buffet style or fill dinner plates in the kitchen. For buffet service, be sure to keep the food hot—use a steam table, if available, electric warming trays, or chafing dishes.

• If using plate service, demonstrate to those who will serve how the finished plates should look. Appoint one person to give each plate a final check, removing any spills with a damp cloth and adding the garnish. It is very important to use standardized portions so there will be enough food for all, yet no wasteful leftovers. To insure accuracy, use standard-size ladles, dippers, or measuring cups for soups, vegetables, and salads. Many of the recipes in this chapter call for the food to be baked in 13x9½x2″ dishes from which you may uniformly cut and serve 6, 8, or 12 squares per pan as needed.

ARROZ CON POLLO

Tender, juicy chicken baked atop bright yellow rice dotted with green peas and pimiento. Such a spectacular dish you'd serve usually to only a few friends. Now, with this recipe, you can impress the whole crowd. Pictured at left.

6 broiler-fryer chickens (2½ to 3 lb. each), cut up	**2 cups chopped onion**
¼ cup olive oil	**4 bay leaves, crumbled**
2 tbsp. salt	**2 tbsp. minced parsley**
1 tbsp. garlic salt	**4 tsp. salt**
2 tsp. pepper	**4 cups uncooked regular rice**
2 tsp. paprika	
6 cans (13¾ oz. each) chicken broth (10 cups)	**3 pkg. (10 oz. each) frozen green peas**
½ tsp. saffron	**4 jars (4 oz. each) pimiento, drained and chopped**

Heat oven to 350°. Place chicken skin side up in four oblong baking pans, 13x9½x2″ each. Brush chicken with oil; sprinkle with 2 tbsp. salt, the garlic salt, pepper, and paprika. Bake 30 min. Heat chicken broth to boiling; add saffron and stir to dissolve. Stir in onion, bay leaves, parsley, and 4 tsp. salt; heat to boiling. Remove the pans from oven; take chicken from pans and set aside. Drain fat from pans. Place 1 cup of rice and ¼ of the boiling chicken broth mixture in each pan; stir until mixed. Top with chicken.

Tightly cover pans with aluminum foil; bake 30 min., or until rice is tender and liquid is absorbed. Remove foil covers and bake 10 min. longer for fluffier rice. Meanwhile, cook peas as directed on package; drain.

To serve, remove chicken pieces from pans. Stir peas and pimiento into rice. Replace chicken pieces on rice mixture. Garnish with parsley and olives, if desired. *24 servings (1 cup rice per portion).*

WILD RICE-CHICKEN CASSEROLE

An elegant party dish combining wild rice, chicken, and mushrooms with creamy and colorful sauce. Remember this for holiday entertaining.

1 cup chicken fat, butter, or margarine	**6 cups cubed cooked chicken or turkey**
1 cup Gold Medal Flour (regular or Wondra)	**3 cans (6 oz. each) sliced mushrooms, drained**
1 tbsp. plus 2 tsp. salt	**1 cup chopped green pepper**
½ tsp. pepper	
3 cups chicken broth*	**1 jar (4 oz.) pimiento, drained and sliced**
4½ cups milk	
4½ cups cooked wild rice	**⅔ cup slivered almonds**

Heat oven to 350°. Melt fat in large heavy saucepot or roaster. Blend in flour, salt, and pepper. Cook over low heat, stirring until mixture is smooth and bubbly. Remove from heat. Stir in chicken broth and milk. Heat to boiling, stirring constantly. Boil 1 min. Add remaining ingredients. Pour into two greased oblong baking dishes, 13x9½x2″ each. Bake 40 to 45 min. If desired, sprinkle with minced parsley before serving. *24 servings (3″ square per portion).*

*Chicken broth may be made by dissolving 3 chicken bouillon cubes in 3 cups boiling water, or use canned chicken broth.

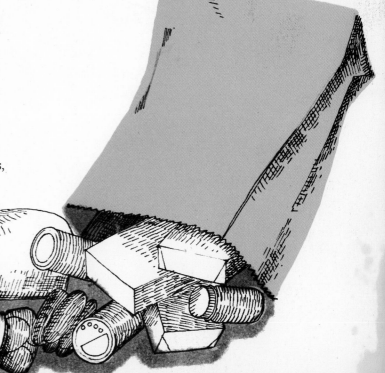

CHUCK WAGON BEANS

1 lb. sliced bacon
6 lb. ground beef
6 cups finely chopped
   onion
2 cups finely chopped
   celery
4 beef bouillon cubes
1⅓ cups boiling water
3 cloves garlic, minced

3 cups catsup
¼ cup plus 2 tbsp.
   prepared mustard
1 tbsp. salt
1 tsp. pepper
4 cans (1 lb. 13 oz. each)
   molasses-style baked
   beans

Heat oven to 375°. Cook bacon until crisp in large heavy roaster; remove and drain on paper towels. Drain bacon fat from the pan. In same pan, cook and stir ground beef, onion and celery until ground beef is browned and onion is tender. Dissolve bouillon cubes in boiling water; stir bouillon and remaining ingredients into meat mixture. Cover; bake 1 hr. 15 min., or until hot and bubbly. Before serving, crumble bacon on top of beans. *24 servings (1 cup per portion).*

HAMBURGER STROGANOFF

4 cans (6 oz. each) sliced
   mushrooms, drained
3 cups finely chopped
   onion
4 cloves garlic, minced
½ cup butter or margarine
4 lb. ground beef
4 cans (10½ oz. each)
   cream of chicken soup

¼ cup Gold Medal Flour
   (regular or Wondra)
4 tsp. salt
1 tsp. pepper
4 cups dairy sour cream
28 oz. noodles, cooked
   and drained
½ cup minced parsley

In heavy Dutch oven or roaster, cook and stir mushrooms, onion, and garlic in butter until onion is almost tender. Add meat and cook until meat is browned. Remove from heat. Mix soup, flour, salt, and pepper; stir soup mixture into meat mixture. Heat to boiling, stirring constantly. Lower heat; cover and simmer 10 min. Stir in sour cream; heat through. Serve meat mixture over hot cooked noodles. Sprinkle with parsley. *24 servings (¾ cup meat mixture per portion).*

Betty Crocker Note: Toss hot drained noodles with a small amount of butter or margarine — a sure way to prevent sticking.

CHILI CON CARNE

Pictured here with Tossed Green Salad (p. 40).

8 lb. ground beef
8 cups chopped onion
8 cans (1 lb. 12 oz. each)
  tomatoes
8 cans (1 lb. each) kidney
  beans, drained (reserve
  liquid)

2 cans (15 oz. each)
  tomato sauce
¼ cup sugar
6 tbsp. chili powder
3 tbsp. salt

Cook and stir ground beef and onion in large heavy roaster until meat is browned and onion is tender. Stir in tomatoes, liquid from kidney beans, tomato sauce, and seasonings. Simmer uncovered 1 hr. 15 min. Add beans and simmer uncovered 15 min., or until of desired consistency. Stir occasionally. *24 servings (1 ½ cups per portion).*

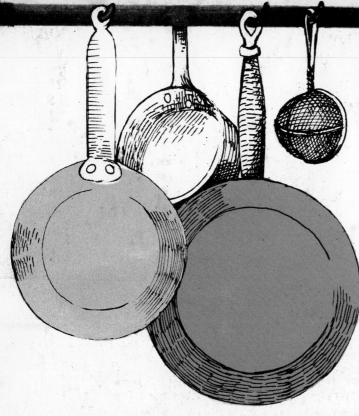

SPARERIBS WITH SAUERKRAUT

Hearty German-type meal that men love! Remember this recipe when planning a father-son banquet.

18 lb. spareribs	2 cups water
4 tsp. salt	4 unpared apples, diced
1 tsp. pepper	4 tbsp. sugar
4 cans (1 lb. 11 oz. each) sauerkraut	4 tsp. caraway seed

Heat oven to 350°. Cut spareribs into 24 serving-size pieces. Place meaty side up on racks in four large heavy Dutch ovens or roasters. Sprinkle with salt and pepper. Bake uncovered 1½ hr., or until spareribs are nicely browned. Take the pans from oven; remove spareribs and racks from pans. Drain off all but 1 tbsp. drippings from each pan. To each pan, add 1 can sauerkraut (with liquid), ½ cup water, ¼ of the apple, 1 tbsp. sugar, and 1 tsp. caraway seed. Mix thoroughly. Top with spareribs. Cover and bake 1 hr., or until spareribs are well done. *24 servings (¾ lb. ribs, ⅔ cup sauerkraut per portion).*

SOUP 'N SAUSAGE CASSEROLE

6 lb. pork sausage	6 envelopes (1¾ oz. each) dehydrated chicken-noodle soup mix
4 cups chopped celery	
2 cups chopped onion	
2 cups chopped green pepper	⅔ cup toasted slivered almonds
4 cups uncooked regular rice	½ tsp. saffron
	3 qt. (12 cups) boiling water

Heat oven to 350°. Form sausage into 48 patties, or if sausage is in rolls, cut into 48 slices. Brown sausage over low heat 10 to 12 min. Remove and drain on paper towels. Drain excess fat from skillet. In same skillet, cook and stir celery, onion, and green pepper until onion is tender. In each of four baking pans, 13x9½x2″, mix ¼ of the onion mixture, 1 cup of the rice, 1½ envelopes of the soup mix, and ¼ of the almonds. Dissolve saffron in boiling water; stir 3 cups of the boiling liquid into each pan. Arrange sausage patties on top. Cover tightly with aluminum foil; bake 45 min., or until rice is tender and liquid absorbed. Trim with parsley, if desired. *24 servings (2 sausage patties and about 4½″ square per portion).*

POTLUCK SCALLOPED POTATOES

6 cans (12 oz. each) pork luncheon meat, cubed, or 9 cups cubed cooked ham	9 cans (10½ oz. each) cream of celery soup
	13 cups thinly sliced pared potatoes (about 8½ lb.)
2¼ cups chopped green pepper	¾ cup dry bread crumbs
2¼ cups chopped onion	1 tbsp. butter or margarine, melted

Heat oven to 350°. Mix meat, green pepper, onion, and soup. In three oblong baking pans, 13x9½x2″ each, layer soup mixture with potatoes (bottom and top layers should be soup mixture). Cover pans with aluminum foil; bake 1½ hr., or until potatoes are tender. Toss bread crumbs with butter. Remove cover from pans; sprinkle with bread crumbs and bake 15 min. *24 servings (about 4½ x3″ portions).*

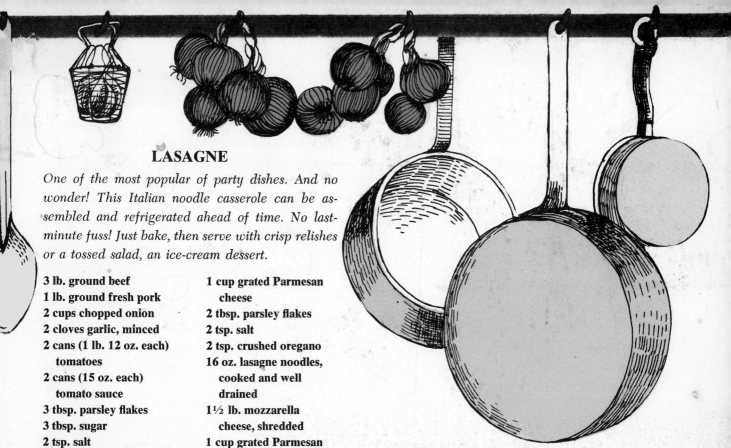

LASAGNE

One of the most popular of party dishes. And no wonder! This Italian noodle casserole can be assembled and refrigerated ahead of time. No last-minute fuss! Just bake, then serve with crisp relishes or a tossed salad, an ice-cream dessert.

3 lb. ground beef
1 lb. ground fresh pork
2 cups chopped onion
2 cloves garlic, minced
2 cans (1 lb. 12 oz. each) tomatoes
2 cans (15 oz. each) tomato sauce
3 tbsp. parsley flakes
3 tbsp. sugar
2 tsp. salt
2 tsp. crushed basil
2 cartons (about 2 lb. each) creamed cottage cheese

1 cup grated Parmesan cheese
2 tbsp. parsley flakes
2 tsp. salt
2 tsp. crushed oregano
16 oz. lasagne noodles, cooked and well drained
1½ lb. mozzarella cheese, shredded
1 cup grated Parmesan cheese

Cook and stir ground beef, ground pork, onion, and garlic in heavy saucepot or roaster until meat is browned and onion is tender. Drain off fat. Add tomatoes and break up with a fork. Stir in tomato sauce, 3 tbsp. parsley flakes, the sugar, 2 tsp. salt, and the basil; simmer uncovered 1 hr., or until mixture is as thick as a good spaghetti sauce.

Heat oven to 350°. Mix cottage cheese, 1 cup Parmesan cheese, 2 tbsp. parsley flakes, 2 tsp. salt, and the oregano. In two oblong baking pans, 13x9½x2″ each, layer half *each* of drained noodles, sauce, mozzarella cheese, and cottage cheese mixture; repeat, reserving enough sauce for thin top layer. Spread sauce over top; sprinkle with 1 cup Parmesan cheese. Bake uncovered 45 min. (Allow additional baking time if casserole has been refrigerated.) Let stand 15 min. after removing from oven. *24 servings (3″ square per portion).*

SHRIMP FRA DIAVOLO

3 cups finely chopped onion
8 cloves garlic, minced
¼ cup olive oil
4 cans (1 lb. each) tomatoes
4 cans (15 oz. each) tomato sauce
½ cup minced parsley

2 tbsp. sugar
1 tbsp. salt
4 tsp. crushed oregano
4 tsp. crushed basil
⅛ tsp. cayenne pepper
3½ to 4 lb. cleaned raw shrimp, fresh or frozen*
48 oz. spaghetti, cooked and drained

Cook and stir onion and garlic in hot oil in large heavy saucepot or roaster until onion is tender. Stir in remaining ingredients except shrimp and spaghetti. Simmer uncovered over low heat 1½ hr., stirring occasionally, or until sauce is thick. Stir in shrimp; cook 10 to 20 min. or until shrimp is pink and tender. Serve with hot spaghetti. *24 servings (1 cup sauce per portion).*

*Run frozen shrimp under cold water to remove ice glaze before adding shrimp to sauce.

CHICKEN PARAGON SALAD

¾ cup lemon juice
10 cups cubed cooked chicken
4 tsp. salt
3 tsp. monosodium glutamate
1½ tsp. sage
½ tsp. pepper
6 cups water
6 chicken bouillon cubes
3 cups uncooked regular rice
2 cups diced green pepper
1 cup diced celery
1 cup sliced green onions and tops
2 jars (4 oz. each) pimiento, drained and chopped
1⅓ cups toasted slivered almonds
2½ cups salad dressing or mayonnaise
⅔ cup milk
4 pkg. (10 oz. each) frozen green peas, cooked, drained, and cooled
Lettuce cups

Drizzle lemon juice over chicken. Sprinkle with salt, monosodium glutamate, sage, and pepper; toss to mix. Cover and refrigerate at least 4 hr.

Combine 6 cups water, bouillon cubes, and rice in large heavy saucepot or Dutch oven. Heat to boiling, stirring once or twice. Lower heat to simmering; cover with tight-fitting lid. Cook 14 min., or until rice is tender and all liquid is absorbed. Remove from heat. Fluff lightly with a fork; let stand in covered pan 10 min. Spread rice on two baking sheets; cover with transparent plastic wrap and chill thoroughly.

Combine chicken (including marinade), green pepper, celery, onions, pimiento, almonds, and chilled rice. Blend salad dressing and milk; fold into chicken mixture. Gently stir in peas. Cover and chill at least 1 hr. Serve in lettuce cups; garnish with lemon and tomato wedges, if desired. *24 servings (1½ cups per portion).*

SALMON BUFFET SALAD

A delightful and economical dish to enhance a luncheon or supper buffet. Serve with a colorful platter of relishes and dark pumpernickel bread.

2½ cups mayonnaise
1 tbsp. salt
1½ tsp. pepper
6 cans (1 lb. each) red salmon, drained
24 oz. macaroni, cooked, drained, and cooled
6 cups diced pared cucumber
½ cup grated onion
½ cup minced parsley
Crisp salad greens

Blend mayonnaise, salt, and pepper. Toss with remaining ingredients except salad greens. Chill well. Serve on crisp salad greens; garnish with lemon wedges, additional minced parsley, and paprika, if desired. *24 servings (1 cup per portion).*

FONDULOHA

A perfect choice for a summer luncheon. Pictured opposite.

6 large fresh pineapples
7½ cups cubed cooked chicken
2½ cups diced celery
2½ cups sliced bananas
1 cup salted peanuts
2½ cups mayonnaise
6 tbsp. chopped chutney, or 1½ tsp. salt and 1 tsp. pepper
1½ to 2 tsp. curry powder
1½ cups shredded or flaked coconut
3 cans (11 oz. each) mandarin orange segments

Leaving green tops on, cut pineapples into fourths lengthwise. Cut around edges with curved knife; remove fruit and cube. Drain fruit and shells on paper towels. Mix pineapple, chicken, celery, bananas, and peanuts. Blend mayonnaise, chutney, and curry powder. Carefully toss mayonnaise mixture with pineapple mixture. Fill each pineapple shell with the fruit mixture. Sprinkle with the coconut. Garnish each with mandarin orange segments. *24 individual pineapple boats.*

CLASSICS FOR A CROWD

COFFEE CLUES . . .

- Always start with a coffee maker that is thoroughly clean.
- Never brew coffee at less than ¾ of the coffee maker's capacity. If a smaller quantity is all that's needed, select a smaller coffee maker.
- Freshness is vital to a good cup of coffee. Use fresh coffee and freshly drawn *cold* water.
- Serve hot steaming coffee as soon as possible after brewing. If necessary to let coffee stand any length of time, hold at serving temperature over very low heat on an asbestos pad. Keep coffee hot but do not boil it.

COFFEE CHART

Average 5½-oz. servings	Measure of Coffee	Amount of Water
20 (for 12 persons)	½ lb.	1 gallon
40 (for 25 persons)	1 lb.	2 gallons

To brew coffee in a saucepot:

Measure "regular" grind coffee into a clean cloth sack; fill only half full to allow for expansion of coffee and free circulation of water. (Before using sack, soak and rinse thoroughly.) Tie sack, allowing enough cord for fastening to pot handle.

In a clean large saucepot, heat measured amount of fresh cold water to a full rolling boil. Reduce heat to hold *just below boiling*. Fasten sack to pot handle; submerge into water. Keep saucepot over low heat. Brew 6 to 8 minutes, pushing sack up and down frequently to get proper extraction. When coffee is ready, remove sack, permitting all extract to drain into saucepot.

To brew coffee in an automatic coffee maker:

Follow manufacturer's directions for selecting grind of coffee, brewing coffee, and holding at serving temperature.

. . . AND TEA TIPS

- Use a spotlessly clean teapot made of glass, china, or earthenware. Rinse the teapot with boiling water and drain.
- Bring freshly drawn cold water to a full rolling boil, then use *immediately*.
- Taste to judge the strength of tea; don't assume strength by the color. Some weak teas produce a dark brew, some strong teas brew to a light tone.

For only a few servings, make tea in a teapot:
Measure tea into teapot, using 1 teaspoon loose tea or 1 tea bag for each cup of tea needed. Pour boiling water over tea and let steep 3 to 5 min. to develop full flavor. Strain tea leaves or remove tea bags. To use instant tea, follow directions on jar.

For 50 portions of tea, prepare a concentrate:
Place 16 family-size tea bags or ¼ lb. loose tea in a large container. Pour 2½ qt. boiling water over tea; steep 5 min. Remove tea bags or strain tea leaves. Using 1 part concentrate to 3 parts boiling water, mix and serve as needed.

TOSSED GREEN SALAD

Crisp and tangy — wonderful accompaniment salad for a dinner in a dish.

3 large heads lettuce	6 tbsp. wine or tarragon vinegar
3 bunches leaf lettuce (about 12 cups)	1 tbsp. salt
1½ small bunches endive (about 3 cups)	3 small cloves garlic, minced
1½ lb. spinach (about 7 cups)	1 tsp. freshly ground pepper
¾ cup olive oil or salad oil (or half each)	1 tsp. monosodium glutamate

Tear greens into bite-size pieces. Toss with oil until leaves glisten. Combine vinegar with remaining seasonings. Toss with greens. Serve immediately.
24 servings (1 cup per portion).

Internationally Inspired

Pizza, Paella, Sukiyaki—each is a distinguished dish in its native land and all are favorites in ours. The list of nations that have contributed great dishes to our American bill of fare lengthens the more we travel, taste, and borrow from the intriguing cuisines of other lands.

Among the recipes in this chapter are great names from the lexicon of cooking, each selected for its natural appeal to the tastes and dining habits of your family and friends. All are freely translated from the famous originals so that their ingredients are locally available and their seasonings are tempered to your liking.

Spread a colorful cloth, set forth your dinner in a dish, and observe the customs of the country in menu, special centerpiece, and setting as you dine adventurously on foreign fare!

England—

Famous for magnificent pies.

ENGLISH STEAK AND KIDNEY PIE

Most popular item on the menu at the famous London chophouse, Ye Olde Cheshire Cheese.

¾ lb. beef or veal kidney	½ lb. fresh mushrooms, sliced, or 1 can (3 oz.) sliced mushrooms
1 tsp. salt	
¾ lb. round steak	¼ cup minced parsley
⅓ cup Gold Medal Flour (regular or Wondra)	¼ cup chopped celery
½ tsp. salt	1 bay leaf
¼ tsp. pepper	1 tsp. salt
1 cup chopped onion	¼ tsp. crushed thyme
¼ cup shortening	¼ tsp. crushed marjoram
½ cup sherry	Dash pepper
½ cup water	Pastry Topping (right)
	⅓ cup cold water
	1 tbsp. flour

Remove skin and membrane from kidney; split in half and remove white veins and fat with kitchen scissors. Cut into 1″ cubes. Cover with water; add 1 tsp. salt and simmer 30 min. Rinse with hot water; drain well. Cut steak into 1″ cubes. Mix ⅓ cup flour, ½ tsp. salt, and ¼ tsp. pepper; roll kidney and steak in flour mixture. Cook and stir meat and onion in hot shortening until meat is brown. Add remaining ingredients except the Pastry Topping, water, and flour. Cover tightly and simmer 1 hr.

Heat oven to 400°. Prepare Pastry Topping. Mix cold water and 1 tbsp. flour; stir into meat mixture. Heat to boiling, stirring constantly. Boil 1 min. Remove bay leaf; pour hot mixture into 1½-qt. casserole. Top with Pastry Topping. Cut slits in pastry and seal to edge of dish. Bake 30 to 35 min., or until crust is browned. *6 servings.*

PASTRY TOPPING

Mix 1¼ cups Gold Medal Flour (regular or Wondra) and ½ tsp. salt in bowl. Cut in ½ cup shortening thoroughly. *Sprinkle* with 3 tbsp. water, a tbsp. at a time, tossing lightly with a fork after each addition. (If dough appears dry, a few drops of water may be added.*) Gather dough into a ball. Turn out onto floured cloth-covered board. Roll out to fit top of casserole, about 8½″ in diameter. (This will be a thick topping.)

*Dough made with Gold Medal Wondra may look and feel different. Work until it holds together.

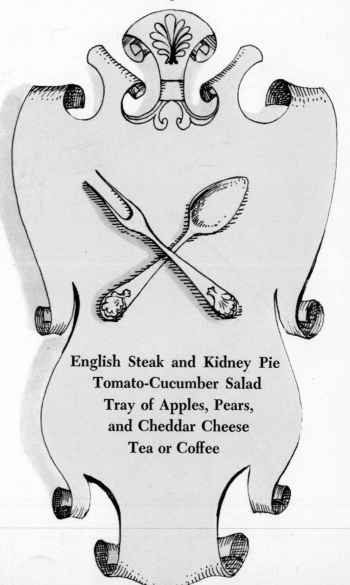

English Steak and Kidney Pie
Tomato-Cucumber Salad
Tray of Apples, Pears,
and Cheddar Cheese
Tea or Coffee

CORNISH PASTIES

1 lb. beef chuck or top round steak, cut into ¼″ pieces
2 cups diced pared potato
2 cups diced carrots
1 cup diced onion
1 cup diced raw turnip or rutabaga

4 sticks of our pie crust mix
2 tsp. salt
Pepper
4 tbsp. butter
Water
Milk or cream
Pickled beets, chili sauce, pickles

Prepare meat and vegetables; set aside. Heat oven to 350°. Prepare pastry as directed on inside wrapper. Gather dough into 4 equal balls. Roll 1 ball into a 12″ circle. Place pastry circle on one end of a large baking sheet. On half of the pastry circle, spread ¼ each of the potatoes and meat; sprinkle with ¼ tsp. salt. On top of the meat, spread in layers ¼ *each* of the carrots, onion, and turnip. Sprinkle with ¼ tsp. salt and dash pepper. Dot with 1 tbsp. butter. Sprinkle 1 tbsp. water over filling. Brush edges of pastry with water. Fold pastry over filling; turn edge of lower pastry over edge of top pastry. Seal and flute. Prick top with fork; brush with milk. Repeat procedure for remaining 3 pasties, placing second pastry circle on other end of baking sheet. Use 2 baking sheets for the 4 pasties. Bake 1 hr. Serve hot or cold with pickled beets, chili sauce, and pickles. *4 servings.*

DINNER IN A PIE CRUST— CORNISH PASTIES

These substantial meat-and-potato turnovers were created expressly to fit into the lunchpails of hard-working Cornishmen and be carried to sea or field or down into the mines of Cornwall.

For your own dinner, serve pasties hot or cold. Our choice is hot, with the pasty cut open and dotted with butter. Always accompany these hearty pies with traditional tart relishes such as pickled beets, chili sauce, and pickles.

CHEDDAR CHEESE PIE

¾ lb. natural sharp Cheddar cheese, shredded (about 3 cups)
1 tsp. instant minced onion
½ tsp. each salt, dry mustard, and Worcestershire sauce

3 eggs
9″ Baked Pie Shell (below)
6 medium tomatoes, peeled and sliced
Salt and pepper
1 to 2 tbsp. chopped green pepper

Heat oven to 325°. In top of double boiler, combine cheese, onion, salt, dry mustard, and Worcestershire sauce. Heat over boiling water, stirring until cheese is melted. Remove from heat. In mixer bowl, beat eggs until frothy. On medium speed, gradually beat cheese mixture into eggs; beat just until smooth. Pour into Baked Pie Shell. Bake 25 min., or until filling is just set. Remove from oven; top with wreath of overlapping tomato slices. Season with salt and pepper. Garnish center with green pepper, if desired. Return to oven and bake 15 min. longer. *6 servings.*

BAKED PIE SHELL

1 cup Gold Medal Flour* (regular or Wondra)
½ tsp. salt

⅓ cup plus 1 tbsp. shortening
2 tbsp. water

Heat oven to 475°. Mix flour and salt. Cut in shortening thoroughly. *Sprinkle* water gradually over mixture, a tbsp. at a time, tossing lightly with a fork after each addition. (If dough appears dry, a few drops of water may be added.) Gather dough into a ball. On lightly floured cloth-covered board, roll 1″ larger than inverted 9″ pie pan. Ease into pan; flute and prick pastry. Bake 8 to 10 min.

*If using Gold Medal Self-Rising Flour, omit salt.

France –

Where cooking with wine is a national art.

BEEF BOURGUIGNONNE

This king of beef stews is accompanied by slices of crusty French bread to be dipped into the sauce.

5 medium onions, sliced	¼ tsp. crushed marjoram
½ lb. fresh mushrooms, sliced	¼ tsp. crushed thyme
2 tbsp. shortening	⅛ tsp. pepper
2 lb. round steak, cut into 1″ cubes	1½ tbsp. flour
	¾ cup beef bouillon*
1 tsp. salt	1½ cups red Burgundy
	Sliced French bread

Cook and stir onions and mushrooms in hot shortening until onion is tender; drain on paper towels. Brown meat in same skillet; add more shortening, as necessary. Remove from heat. Sprinkle seasonings over meat. Mix flour and bouillon; pour into skillet. Heat to boiling, stirring constantly. Boil 1 min. Stir in Burgundy. Cover; simmer until meat is tender, 1½ to 2 hr. The liquid should always just cover the meat. (If necessary, add a little more bouillon and Burgundy—1 part bouillon to 2 parts Burgundy.) Gently stir in onions and mushrooms; cook uncovered 15 min., or until heated through. Serve in large soup bowls or individual casseroles. Sprinkle with minced parsley, if desired. Serve with French bread. *4 servings.*

*Beef bouillon may be made by dissolving 1 beef bouillon cube in ¾ cup boiling water, or use canned beef broth.

A TEMPTING TOPPING

For wonderful flavor, mix seedless green grapes with dairy sour cream; sprinkle with brown sugar and chill. Serve spooned over wedges of chiffon cake or melon.

Beef Bourguignonne
French Bread
Romaine-Radish Salad
Sour Cream and Green Grapes
with Chiffon Cake or Melon

COQ AU VIN

Chicken in red wine—elegant fare borrowed from the French cuisine! Long simmering blends the wine and herb flavors, lets them penetrate deep into the chicken.

¼ cup Gold Medal Flour (regular or Wondra)
½ tsp salt
¼ tsp. pepper
3- to 3½-lb. broiler-fryer chicken, cut up
6 slices bacon
6 small onions
½ lb. fresh mushrooms, sliced
4 carrots, halved
1 cup chicken broth*
1 cup red Burgundy
1 clove garlic, crushed
½ tsp. salt
Bouquet Garni (below)

Mix flour, salt, and pepper; coat chicken with mixture. In large skillet or Dutch oven, fry bacon until crisp; remove and drain on paper towels. Brown chicken well in hot bacon drippings; push chicken aside. Add onions and mushrooms; cook and stir until onions are tender. Drain off the fat. Crumble and add bacon. Stir in remaining ingredients. Cover and simmer 1 hr. 15 min., or until chicken is tender. Remove Bouquet Garni before serving. Skim off excess fat. Serve chicken sprinkled with minced parsley, if desired. *4 to 6 servings.*

*Chicken broth may be made by dissolving 1 chicken bouillon cube in 1 cup boiling water, or use canned chicken broth.

Betty Crocker Note: To skim off fat quickly and easily, slightly cool entire mixture. Skim off fat. Reheat to serving temperature.

BOUQUET GARNI

Tie ½ tsp. crushed thyme, 1 bay leaf, and 2 large sprigs parsley in cheesecloth bag or place them in a tea ball.

Coq au Vin
French Bread
Tossed Salad with French Dressing (p. 122)
Cream Puffs or Éclairs
Coffee

CRÊPES VERSAILLES

Thin, delicate crêpes filled with a rich chicken-mushroom sauce and topped with melted Swiss cheese. As elegant a dish as you could hope to serve—worthy of raves at a ladies' luncheon!

Crêpes (below)
Filling (below)
Cream Sauce (right)

1 cup shredded Swiss cheese
Nutmeg

Prepare Crêpes, Filling, and Cream Sauce. Heat oven to 350°. Spoon Filling onto each crêpe; roll up. Place in shallow baking dish. Cover with Cream Sauce and sprinkle with cheese and nutmeg. Bake 20 min., or until the center is hot. *4 to 6 servings.*

CRÊPES

1 cup Bisquick
1 egg

1 cup milk

Beat Bisquick, egg, and milk with rotary beater until smooth. Lightly grease 6 or 7″ round skillet. Pour scant ¼ cupful into hot skillet. Tilt the pan to coat bottom. Bake until bubbles appear. Turn pancake gently and finish baking. Repeat, making 12 to 18 pancakes. Place baked pancakes between folds of towel until ready to use.

FILLING

1 can (2 oz.) mushrooms, drained
¼ cup chopped green pepper
¼ cup butter or margarine
¼ cup Gold Medal Flour (regular or Wondra)

1 tsp. salt
⅛ tsp. pepper
1 cup chicken broth*
1 cup light cream
1 cup diced cooked chicken
¼ cup chopped pimiento

Cook and stir mushrooms and green pepper in butter. Remove from heat. Blend in flour, salt, and pepper. Cook, stirring until mixture is bubbly. Remove from heat. Stir in chicken broth and cream; heat to boiling, stirring constantly. Boil 1 min. Mix in chicken and pimiento; heat through.

*Chicken broth may be made by dissolving 1 chicken bouillon cube in 1 cup boiling water, or use canned chicken broth.

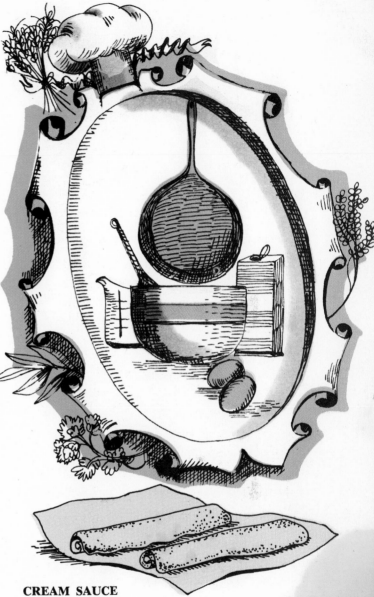

CREAM SAUCE

Melt 1 tbsp. butter over low heat in saucepan. Blend in 1 tbsp. flour. Cook over low heat, stirring until mixture is smooth and bubbly. Remove from heat. Stir in 1 cup light cream. Heat to boiling, stirring constantly. Boil 1 min.

Variation: Prepare Cream Sauce as directed above except—reduce cream to ¾ cup and add 2 tbsp. sherry. Omit nutmeg.

Germany–
The influence of cabbage and caraway.

SAUERBRATEN DINNER

3½- to 4-lb. beef chuck
   roast
2 onions, sliced
2 bay leaves
12 peppercorns
6 whole cloves
12 juniper berries, if desired
2 tsp. salt
1½ cups red wine vinegar

1 cup boiling water
2 tbsp. shortening
1 medium head (about
   2 lb.) red cabbage,
   cut into 8 wedges
Caraway Dumplings
   (below)
12 gingersnaps, crushed
2 tsp. sugar

Place roast in an earthenware bowl with onions, seasonings, vinegar, and boiling water; cover. Marinate 3 days or more in refrigerator; turn meat twice a day with two wooden spoons. (Never pierce meat with a fork.)

Drain meat. Brown on all sides in hot shortening in heavy skillet. Add marinade mixture; cover and simmer slowly 2½ to 3 hr., or until meat is tender. Remove meat and onions; keep warm. Strain and measure liquid; add water, if needed, to make 2½ cups liquid. Pour liquid back into skillet; add cabbage wedges. Cover and simmer 10 min. Stir gingersnaps and sugar into liquid; simmer gently 3 min. longer.

Prepare Caraway Dumplings; spoon onto cabbage. (Be sure liquid is bubbling; the steam helps them rise. Drop dough onto cabbage, not into liquid.) Cook uncovered over low heat 10 min.; cover and cook 10 min. longer. Liquid should just bubble gently. Serve meat, cabbage wedges, and dumplings on a platter; accompany with gingersnap gravy. 8 *servings.*

CARAWAY DUMPLINGS

Mix 2 cups Bisquick, 1½ tsp. caraway seed, and ¾ cup milk thoroughly with a fork.

Sauerbraten with Cabbage and
Caraway Dumplings
Apple-Grape Salad
Cheesecake with Cherry Sauce
Coffee

Italy — *Pizza and pasta and everything good!*

OLD COUNTRY ITALIAN SPAGHETTI

2 cans (1 lb. 4 oz. each) tomatoes
1 can (6 oz.) tomato paste
1 cup water
1 tsp. crushed basil
⅛ tsp. crushed oregano
⅛ tsp. red pepper
1½ tsp. salt
¼ tsp. black pepper
Meatballs (below)
14 to 16 oz. long spaghetti, cooked and drained

Combine all ingredients except the Meatballs and spaghetti in large heavy skillet. Simmer uncovered 1 hr., stirring occasionally. Add Meatballs to sauce; cover and simmer 20 min. Serve over hot spaghetti. *8 servings.*

MEATBALLS

1½ lb. ground beef
¼ lb. ground pork
1 cup fine dry bread crumbs
1 clove garlic, minced
½ cup milk
½ cup grated Parmesan cheese
⅓ cup chopped onion
1 egg, beaten
1 tbsp. minced parsley
½ tsp. salt
¼ tsp. pepper
⅛ tsp. each cinnamon, allspice, and nutmeg
¼ tsp. lemon juice
⅛ tsp. each crushed basil and oregano
⅛ tsp. red pepper
¼ cup olive oil

Thoroughly mix all ingredients except olive oil. Shape mixture into 1″ balls; brown in hot oil in heavy skillet. Remove meatballs and drain on paper towels.

Betty Crocker Note: After Meatballs have been added to the sauce, stir carefully so balls will not break apart.

WHIPPED CREAM TOPPER
Beat ½ cup whipping cream and 1 tsp. sugar until stiff. Fold in 2 to 3 tsp. sherry, cointreau, or kirsch. *Makes 1 cup.*

Antipasto Tray
Old Country Italian Spaghetti
Fresh Mushroom Tossed Salad
Hard Rolls
Fruit Tarts with Whipped Cream Topper

ANTIPASTO TRAY

For an attractive appetizer, arrange your choice of the following on a bed of endive:

  Salami strips or pepperoni cuts
  Assorted Italian cheeses
  Prosciutto (spicy Italian-style ham)
  Green or ripe olives
  Pickled artichoke hearts
  Italian peppers
  Celery stuffed with anchovy cream cheese

Serve with small thin rounds of bread, sprinkled with Parmesan cheese and oven-toasted.

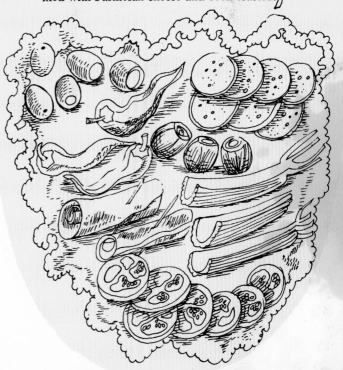

PIZZA

- 1 pkg. active dry yeast
- ¾ cup warm water (105 to 115°)
- 2½ cups Bisquick
- ¾ cup chopped onion
- 1 clove garlic, minced
- 1 can (15 oz.) tomato sauce
- 1 cup sliced pepperoni or cooked Italian sausage or 2 cans anchovies, chopped
- ½ tsp. salt
- ¼ tsp. pepper
- 2½ cups shredded mozzarella cheese or 2 pkg. (6 oz. each) sliced mozzarella cheese, cut into thin strips
- 3 to 4 tsp. crushed oregano

Heat oven to 425°. Dissolve yeast in warm water. Add Bisquick and beat vigorously. Turn dough onto well-floured surface. Knead until smooth, about 20 times. Allow dough to rest a few min. Divide dough into 4 parts. Roll each piece paper-thin into a circle, about 10″ in diameter. Place on ungreased baking sheets. Pinch edge of dough to make a slight rim.

Mix onion, garlic, tomato sauce, meat, salt, and pepper; spread on dough. Sprinkle with shredded cheese or arrange cheese strips on top. Sprinkle with oregano to desired amount. Bake 15 to 20 min., or until crust is brown and filling hot and bubbly. Cut into pie-shaped wedges; serve immediately. *4 servings.*

HAMBURGER PIZZA

Follow recipe at left except — substitute 1 lb. browned ground beef and ½ cup chopped green pepper for the meat.

TUNA PIZZA

Follow recipe at left except—substitute 1 can (6½ oz. or 9¼ oz.) tuna, drained and flaked, and 1 can (8 oz.) sliced mushrooms, cooked in butter, for meat. Omit the garlic.

VEAL SCALLOPINI

1½ to 2 lb. veal steak,
 ½″ thick
Salt and pepper
2 tbsp. salad oil
1 pkg. of our noodles
 Italiano

¾ cup hot water
1 can (3 oz.) sliced
 mushrooms, undrained
2 tbsp. butter or margarine
¼ cup hot water

Cut veal into 4 serving-size pieces. Sprinkle with salt and pepper; brown in hot oil. Stir together tomato sauce mix from noodles Italiano, ¾ cup water, and mushrooms; pour over meat. Cover; simmer 45 min., or until meat is tender. Cook and drain noodles as directed on package. Stir in butter, cheese mix, and ¼ cup water. Arrange meat and noodles on platter. Top with sauce. *4 servings.*

ROUND 'N RAVIOLI

A flavorful combination of round steak, Italian-style squash, and canned convenience foods. Easy to assemble!

3 tbsp. flour
½ tsp. crushed oregano
1 tsp. salt
¼ tsp. pepper
1½ lb. round steak,
 1½″ thick
1 tbsp. shortening

1 can (15½ oz.) spaghetti
 sauce with mushrooms
1 can (1 lb.) small whole
 white onions, drained
3 medium zucchini
 squash (about ¾ lb.),
 halved lengthwise
1 can (15½ oz.) cheese
 ravioli in sauce

Heat oven to 375°. Mix flour and seasonings; coat meat with this mixture. (Reserve remaining flour.) Brown meat in hot shortening. Place in oblong baking dish, 11½x7½x1½″. Drain off excess fat. Add spaghetti sauce to same skillet and stir in reserved flour mixture. Heat to boiling, stirring constantly. Pour over meat; cover with aluminum foil. Bake 45 min. Uncover; place onions and squash in sauce around meat, spooning some sauce over the vegetables. Spoon ravioli and sauce over meat. Cover; bake 45 min., or until meat is tender and squash is done. *6 servings.*

CHICKEN CACCIATORE

¼ cup Gold Medal Flour
 (regular or Wondra)
1 tsp. salt
2½- to 3-lb. broiler-fryer
 chicken, cut up
¼ cup olive oil or
 salad oil
1 green pepper, cut into
 strips
2 medium onions,
 quartered

1 can (15 oz.) tomato
 sauce
½ cup water
1 clove garlic, minced
1 tsp. salt
1 tsp. crushed oregano
¼ tsp. pepper
¼ tsp. crushed thyme
1 can (4 oz.) mushroom
 stems and pieces
3 cups hot cooked rice

Mix flour and 1 tsp. salt; coat chicken pieces with mixture. Brown chicken on both sides in hot oil, about 20 min.; drain well on paper towels. Drain excess fat from skillet. Return chicken to skillet; add green pepper and onion. Mix tomato sauce, water, seasonings, and mushrooms (with liquid); pour over chicken. Cover and simmer 45 min., or until chicken is tender. Serve over hot cooked rice. *4 servings.*

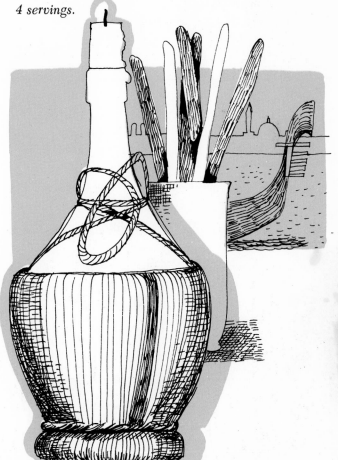

Spain—*Traditional dishes seasoned with finesse.*

Paella Valenciana
Sliced Orange Salad
Caramel Custard

PAELLA VALENCIANA

2½- to 3-lb. broiler-fryer chicken, cut into serving-size pieces
¼ cup olive oil
8 onion slices (⅛″ thick)
3 cups cut-up fresh tomatoes (4 medium)
1½ cups uncooked regular rice
3 cups chicken broth*
2 tbsp. paprika
2 tbsp. salt
½ tsp. pepper
¼ tsp. cayenne pepper
⅛ tsp. saffron

2 cups cleaned cooked or canned shrimp
1 lb. fresh or frozen fish fillets (such as haddock or pike), cubed
1 can (5 oz.) lobster, drained and cartilage removed
1 pkg. (10 oz.) frozen green peas, broken apart
1 can (15 oz.) artichoke hearts, drained
1 jar (4 oz.) sliced pimiento, drained

In Dutch oven or heavy kettle, brown chicken in hot oil; remove chicken. Drain off fat. Add onion and tomatoes; cook 5 min., or until onion is tender. Stir in rice, broth, and seasonings. Add browned chicken; cover tightly and simmer 20 min. Gently stir in shrimp, fish, lobster, and peas. Cover and simmer 15 min. more. Carefully stir in artichoke hearts and pimiento; heat through. Serve in large shallow dish. Garnish with parsley, if desired. *8 servings.*

*Chicken broth may be made by dissolving 3 chicken bouillon cubes in 3 cups boiling water, or use canned chicken broth.

SPANISH VEAL

1½ lb. boneless veal shoulder, cut into 1½″ cubes
¼ cup shortening
1 tsp. salt
⅛ tsp. pepper
1 bay leaf, crumbled
1 clove garlic, minced

1 tbsp. minced onion
1 can (16 oz.) tomatoes
1 cup water
1 can (1 lb.) cut green beans, drained
2 tbsp. flour
½ cup cold water

Brown meat on all sides in hot shortening. Stir in salt, pepper, bay leaf, garlic, onion, tomatoes, and 1 cup water. Cover tightly; simmer 1¼ hr. Add green beans; heat to boiling, reduce heat and simmer 5 to 10 min., or until beans are hot. Mix flour and ½ cup cold water; stir into meat mixture. Heat to boiling, stirring constantly. Boil 1 min. *4 to 6 servings.*

Mexico—*Land of lively, tantalizing flavors.*

Sombrero Pie
Avocado-Orange Salad
Ripe and Green Olives
Scoops of Assorted Fruit Sherbets
Chocolate Sauce   Coffee

SOMBRERO PIE

½ lb. ground beef	1 can (12 oz.) whole kernel
½ lb. ground fresh pork	corn, drained, or 1 pkg.
1 large onion, sliced	(10 oz.) frozen corn
1 can (1 lb. 4 oz.)	1 to 2 tbsp. chili powder
tomato juice	1 tsp. salt
	¼ tsp. pepper
	Cornmeal Pastry (right)

Heat oven to 400°. Cook and stir meat and onion in large skillet until onion is tender and meat is browned. Stir in tomato juice, corn, and seasonings. Simmer 10 min. Pour bubbly hot meat mixture into oblong baking dish, 11½x7½x1½". Cover with pastry. Bake 30 to 35 min. *4 to 6 servings.*

CORNMEAL PASTRY

1¼ cups Gold Medal Flour	1 tsp. salt
(regular or Wondra)	½ cup salad oil
½ cup cornmeal	3 tbsp. cold water

Mix flour, cornmeal, and salt. Mix in oil until mixture looks like fine crumbs. Sprinkle with water and mix with fork. Press firmly into a ball. If too dry to form ball, work in 1 to 2 tbsp. more oil. Roll pastry between two sheets of waxed paper into a rectangle, 12x7". Peel off top paper and invert pastry on meat mixture. Peel off second piece of waxed paper; cut 3 or 4 slits near center of pastry.

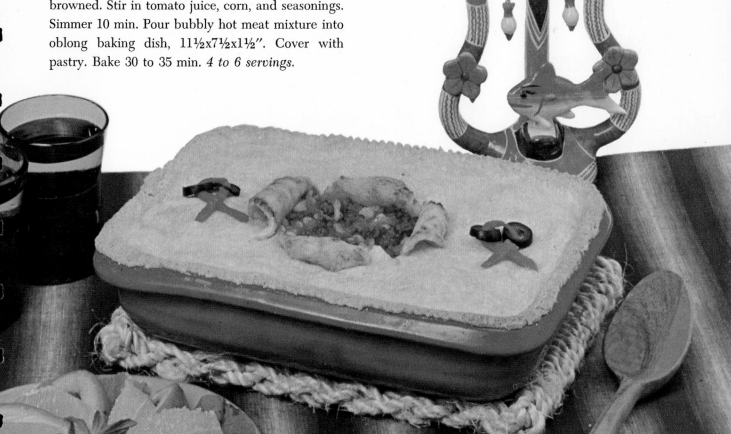

Africa — *Exotic combinations of familiar foods.*

GOLD COAST STEW

2 green peppers, cut into rings	1½ tsp. salt
1 medium onion, cut into rings	1 tsp. chili powder
	1 tsp. sugar
2 tbsp. shortening	½ tsp. nutmeg
1 can (6 oz.) tomato paste	4 cups cubed cooked chicken
¾ cup peanut butter	6 cups hot cooked rice
3 cups chicken broth*	Accompaniments (right)

Cook and stir green pepper and onion in hot shortening until onion is tender. Drain off excess fat. In a bowl, blend tomato paste and peanut butter; stir in broth and seasonings; add to onion mixture. Stir in chicken. Cook and stir over low heat until heated through. (If too thick, stir in more chicken broth.) Serve over hot rice with your choice of Accompaniments. *8 servings.*

*Chicken broth may be made by dissolving 3 chicken bouillon cubes in 3 cups boiling water, or use canned chicken broth.

Gold Coast Stew
Watermelon Pickles
Date Pudding   Hot Coffee

ACCOMPANIMENTS
Grated coconut
Chopped peanuts
Pineapple chunks
Sautéed banana slices (¼″ thick)
Sautéed tomato slices
Sautéed eggplant slices

India — *Triumphant curries of lamb, fowl, and seafood.*

CHICKEN MADRAS

1 tart apple, pared and diced
1 cup cooked diced carrots
1 stalk celery, diced
2 small onions, chopped
1 clove garlic, minced
¼ cup butter or margarine
2 tbsp. flour
1 tsp. curry powder
1 tsp. salt
½ tsp. dry mustard
⅛ tsp. sage
1½ cups chicken broth*
1 bay leaf
3 cups diced cooked chicken
½ cup light cream
2 tbsp. chopped chutney
Rice Ring (p. 141)
Curry Accompaniments (right)

Cook and stir apple, carrots, celery, onions, and garlic in butter 5 min. Remove from heat. Mix flour with curry powder, salt, mustard, and sage; stir into butter mixture. Cook, stirring until mixture is bubbly. Remove from heat. Stir in chicken broth. Add bay leaf. Heat to boiling, stirring constantly. Boil 1 min. Stir in chicken, cream, and chutney; heat through. Remove bay leaf. Serve in Rice Ring. Pass Curry Accompaniments. *4 to 6 servings.*

*Chicken broth may be made by dissolving 1 to 2 chicken bouillon cubes in 1½ cups boiling water, or use canned chicken broth.

HENNY PENNY HINT

Know the right way to stew a chicken—see p. 144. It adds up to more flavor for any dinner in a dish with cooked chicken as a key ingredient.

Chicken Madras
Curry Accompaniments
Bowl of Fruit
Hot Tea

NOODLE RING WITH CALCUTTA CHICKEN

1 pkg. of our noodles almondine
1 tbsp. butter or margarine
1 egg, slightly beaten
½ cup milk
½ cup raisins
Calcutta Chicken (below)
Curry Accompaniments (below)

Heat oven to 350°. Cook and drain noodles as directed on package for range-top method. Stir in all ingredients except Calcutta Chicken and Curry Accompaniments. Pour into well-buttered 1-qt. ring mold. Place in pan of hot water, 1″ deep. Bake 30 min., or until silver knife inserted into center comes out clean. To unmold, run spatula around edge; invert on serving plate and shake gently. Fill center with Calcutta Chicken. Serve with the almonds and Curry Accompaniments. *4 servings.*

CALCUTTA CHICKEN

½ cup diced celery
2 tbsp. butter or margarine
½ tsp. curry powder
1½ cups milk
1 cup cubed cooked chicken

Cook and stir celery in butter for 5 min. Remove from heat. Blend in curry powder, packet of seasoned sauce mix from package of noodles almondine, and milk. Simmer 8 to 10 min., stirring occasionally. Stir in chicken; heat through.

CURRY ACCOMPANIMENTS

Choose 6 or 7 accompaniments and serve in small bowls. Chutney is the most popular and a must for true curry fans!

Chutney
Plumped raisins
Chopped salted peanuts or slivered almonds
Sieved hard-cooked eggs
Flaked coconut
Chopped crystallized ginger
Pineapple chunks
Crisp bacon bits
Currant jelly

China—*Superbly simple cooking for delicate natural tastes.*

LAMB CHOPS WITH CHINESE VEGETABLES

Serve with a salad of mandarin oranges, and for fun, end the meal with Chinese fortune cookies.

4 shoulder lamb chops, 1″ thick	1 clove garlic, minced
1 can (1 lb.) Chinese vegetables	2 beef bouillon cubes
1 can (5 oz.) water chestnuts, sliced very thinly	1 medium onion, sliced
	2 tbsp. cornstarch
3 tbsp. soy sauce	¼ cup cold water
	1 green pepper, cut into ⅛″ strips
	4 cherry tomatoes

Trim excess fat from chops; lightly grease heavy skillet with fat from one chop. Brown meat on both sides. Drain off excess fat. Drain liquid from Chinese vegetables and water chestnuts, reserving ¾ cup liquid. Mix reserved liquid, soy sauce, garlic, and bouillon cubes; pour into skillet. Heat and stir to dissolve bouillon cubes; add onion. Cover and simmer 30 min., or until chops are tender. Remove meat from skillet. Blend cornstarch with cold water; stir slowly into liquid in skillet. Cook, stirring constantly, until mixture thickens and boils. Boil and stir 1 min. Stir in green pepper, Chinese vegetables, and water chestnuts; add chops and cherry tomatoes. Cover and simmer 10 min. *4 servings.*

CHOW MEIN

1 lb. lean pork steak	1 can (3 oz.) sliced mushrooms, drained (reserve ¼ cup liquid)
1 cup sliced celery	
½ cup chopped onion	
3 tbsp. soy sauce	1 can (1 lb.) Chinese vegetables, drained
1 tsp. monosodium glutamate	
	2 tbsp. brown gravy sauce (bead molasses type)
2 cups beef bouillon*	
3 tbsp. cornstarch	3 cups chow mein noodles

Trim excess fat from meat. Cut meat diagonally into paper-thin slices. Lightly grease large skillet with the trimmed fat. Brown meat on both sides. Stir in celery, onion, soy sauce, monosodium glutamate, and bouillon. Cover and simmer 30 min. Blend cornstarch with reserved mushroom liquid; slowly stir into mixture in skillet. Add mushrooms, Chinese vegetables, and bead molasses. Cook, stirring constantly, until mixture thickens and boils. Boil and stir 1 min. Serve over chow mein noodles. *4 servings.*

*Beef bouillon may be made by dissolving 2 beef bouillon cubes in 2 cups boiling water, or used canned beef broth.

**Egg Rolls
with Hot Mustard and Red Sauce
Barbecued Spareribs
Chinese Beef and Pea Pods
Rice
Almond or Fortune Cookies
Hot Tea**

CHINESE BEEF AND PEA PODS

Pictured below.

1 lb. beef tenderloin or
    sirloin steak
Soy sauce
4 slices fresh ginger root,
    smashed and cut into
    pieces
Salt
Monosodium glutamate
Garlic powder
½ lb sugar pea pods or
    1 pkg. (10 oz.) frozen
    sugar pea pods
Salad oil
¼ lb. fresh mushrooms,
    sliced

3 stalks Chinese cabbage,
    cut diagonally into ¼″
    slices (2 cups)
¼ cup instant minced
    onion
1 can (5 oz.) water
    chestnuts, drained and
    sliced paper-thin
1 can (5 oz.) bamboo
    shoots, drained
1 can (13¾ oz.) chicken
    broth
1 tbsp. cornstarch
¼ tsp. sugar
2 green onions, thinly
    sliced

Cut meat diagonally into paper-thin slices. Mix 1 tbsp. soy sauce, 1 slice ginger root, ¼ tsp. salt, ⅛ tsp. monosodium glutamate, and ⅛ tsp. garlic powder in bowl. Toss meat thoroughly in soy mixture; let stand 1 hr. Cook pea pods in boiling water 1 min.; drain.

Lightly grease skillet or wok pan with 1 tbsp. salad oil; add the marinated meat and 1 slice ginger root. Brown meat lightly on both sides; remove. In the same skillet, heat 2 tbsp. salad oil; add mushrooms, Chinese cabbage, minced onion, water chestnuts, bamboo shoots, and 2 slices ginger root. Cook 2 min., tossing constantly. Stir in ½ cup of the chicken broth, ¼ cup soy sauce, 1 tsp. salt, ½ tsp. monosodium glutamate, and ⅛ tsp. garlic powder. Cover and simmer 3 min. Blend cornstarch with sugar, ¼ tsp. monosodium glutamate, 1 tsp. soy sauce, and remaining chicken broth; stir into skillet. Cook, stirring constantly, until mixture thickens and boils. Boil and stir 1 min. Add meat and pea pods; heat through, but do not overcook. Place in large bowl; garnish with green onions. Serve over rice, if desired. *4 servings.*

Good Chinese cooks smash a thin slice of ginger with the broad side of a heavy knife. This releases flavor, but not the juices. If your knives are not heavy enough, place ginger slice between waxed paper and pound evenly with wooden mallet or back of flat wooden spoon.

Japan—*Subtly flavored foods*.

SUKIYAKI

1 lb. round steak
1 tbsp. salad oil
½ lb. mushrooms, thinly sliced
1 bunch green onions, cut into 1½″ lengths
3 stalks celery, sliced
2 large onions, thinly sliced

1 can (5 oz.) bamboo shoots, drained
3 tbsp. sugar
⅓ cup soy sauce
1 chicken bouillon cube dissolved in ½ cup hot water
3 cups raw spinach leaves, washed
3 cups hot cooked rice

Cut round steak into strips, 2x¼″; brown in hot oil. Add remaining ingredients except spinach and rice. Simmer uncovered until vegetables are tender, about 10 min. Add spinach; cook 5 min. Serve over rice. *4 servings.*

Sukiyaki   Rice
Cucumber-Crab Salad
Honeydew Melon or Strawberries

Polynesia — *Typically tropical flavors, light and satisfying.*

POLYNESIAN PORK 'N PINEAPPLE

6 pork chops
Salt and pepper
1 can (13½ oz.)
  pineapple chunks,
  drained
1 large onion, chopped
¼ cup minced celery
  leaves

1 clove garlic, minced
12 cooked prunes, pitted
2 tbsp. soy sauce
½ tsp. crushed marjoram
1 cup diagonally sliced
  celery
Fluffy Ginger Rice
  (below)

Trim excess fat from chops; lightly grease heavy skillet with fat from one chop. Brown chops on both sides. Season lightly with salt and pepper. Drain off excess fat. Add remaining ingredients except celery and rice. Cover and simmer over medium heat 20 to 30 min. Add celery and cook 10 min. longer, or until celery is crisp-tender and pork is well done—no pink in center. (If mixture is too dry, add a small amount of water.) Serve over Fluffy Ginger Rice. *6 servings.*

FLUFFY GINGER RICE

Prepare 1 cup uncooked regular rice as directed on p. 140 except—add 1 tsp. cut-up crystallized ginger before cooking.

**Polynesian Pork 'n Pineapple
Spinach Tossed Salad
Banana Cake with Coconut Frosting**

ISLAND SKILLET DINNER

½ cup water
1 tsp. salt
1 lb. fresh whole green
  beans (remove ends)
1 cup diagonally sliced
  celery
1 medium green pepper,
  sliced into strips,
  ⅓″ wide

1 lb. sliced cooked
  turkey or chicken
1½ cups cherry tomatoes
1 can (1 lb. 4 oz.)
  pineapple spears,
  drained (reserve syrup)
1 ripe banana
Oriental Sauce (below)
3 to 4 cups hot cooked
  rice

Heat water and salt to boiling in large skillet; place beans on one side, the celery and green pepper on the other side. Cook uncovered 5 min. Cover tightly and simmer 20 to 25 min., or until beans are tender. Push beans and the celery and pepper mixture into 2 pie-shaped wedges in skillet. Add turkey, tomatoes, and pineapple spears, also arranging each in a pie-shaped wedge. Slice banana over pineapple spears. Pour Oriental Sauce over all. Cover and simmer 10 to 15 min., or until heated through. Serve with hot rice. *4 to 6 servings.*

ORIENTAL SAUCE

¾ cup brown sugar
  (packed)
3 tbsp. cornstarch
¾ cup cold water
⅓ cup vinegar

Reserved pineapple
  syrup
3 tbsp. light molasses
2 chicken bouillon cubes

Mix ingredients in saucepan; cook, stirring constantly, until mixture thickens and boils. Boil and stir 1 min.

ALAMO TAMALE SUPPER

Quick-as-ever Mexican supper dish.

½ cup chopped onion	1 can (8 oz.) tomato sauce
1 tbsp. shortening	
1 can (1 lb.) beef tamales in sauce	1 tsp. chili powder
	1 cup shredded sharp Cheddar cheese
1 can (8 oz.) whole kernel corn	¼ cup sliced pitted ripe olives

Heat oven to 350°. In a medium skillet with oven-proof handle, cook and stir onion in hot shortening until tender. Remove from heat; stir in sauce from tamales, the corn (including liquid), tomato sauce, and chili powder. Simmer uncovered 5 min. Stir in *half* the cheese. Remove papers from tamales; arrange spoke-fashion in skillet. Sprinkle olives and remaining cheese in a circle in center. Cover and bake 15 min., or just until tamales are heated and sauce is bubbly. *4 servings.*

CURRIED NOODLES ROMANOFF

1 pkg. of our noodles Romanoff	½ cup diced celery
	½ tsp. curry powder
1½ cups cut-up cooked pork, chicken, or lamb	

Heat oven to 350°. Prepare noodles Romanoff as directed on package except—use only ⅔ cup milk. Stir in the remaining ingredients. Pour into 1½-qt. casserole. Cover; bake 15 min. *4 servings.*

EASY ITALIAN SPAGHETTI

½ lb. ground beef	1 tsp. sugar
⅓ cup chopped onion	7 or 8 oz. long spaghetti, cooked and drained
1 can (8 oz.) tomato sauce	
1 can (10¾ oz.) spaghetti sauce with mushrooms	Grated sharp American or Parmesan cheese

Cook and stir ground beef and onion in skillet until onion is tender and meat is browned. Stir in sauces and sugar. Heat to boiling; reduce heat and simmer 5 min. Pour over hot cooked spaghetti on platter. Sprinkle with cheese. *3 to 4 servings.*

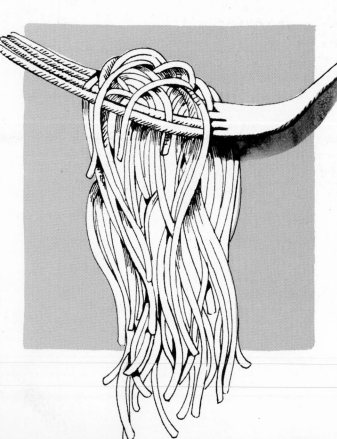

INSTANT-ITALY MEATBALLS

½ lb. ground beef	1 pkg. of our noodles Italiano
¼ cup crushed Wheaties or cornflakes	
	2 tbsp. shortening
1 tbsp. minced parsley	1⅓ cups hot water
1 egg	

Heat oven to 375°. Mix ground beef, crushed cereal, parsley, egg, and cheese mix from noodles Italiano. Shape mixture into 1″ balls; brown in hot shortening. Cook and drain noodles as directed on package; combine with meatballs in a 1½-qt. casserole. Stir water and tomato sauce mix together; pour over noodles and meatballs. Bake 20 min. *4 servings.*

Fast and Flavorful

In the busy, whizzing life we lead these days, who doesn't want new ways to serve maximum meals in minimum time?

Take stock of today's wealth of modern mixes, of the canned, dried, and frozen specialties, and the soups of all kinds on your supermarket shelves. These 20th-century convenience foods, with the special seasoning and much of the time-consuming preparation already done for you, offer help in everyday meal planning and first aid when an emergency turns the dinner hour topsy-turvy or when unexpected guests come to call.

Do as we've done—combine foods that cook with speed in oven, skillet, or broiler to make complete meals in one. All of these recipes will lighten your work load. Every one is easy, fast, and as modern as today. And the results taste as good as Grandmother's. Maybe better!

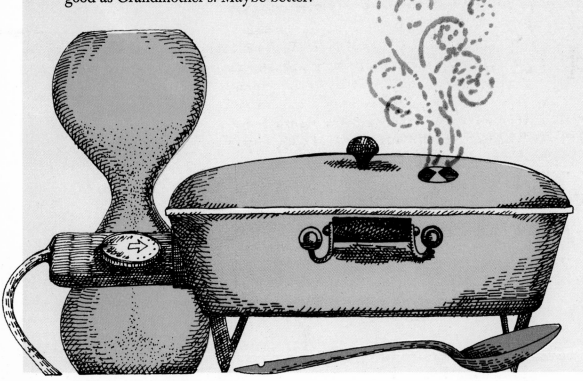

Oven Quick

Many casseroles in this section bake in 30 minutes—or less! You can work or play almost until the dinner hour, then whisk into the kitchen to put your meal together in a twinkling.

For greater efficiency, call on quick-to-fix breads and desserts to complete your menu; those that can share the oven with your casserole are best, of course. Keep on hand a supply of mixes for gingerbread, brownies, cookies, cakes, and pastry; also canned and frozen fruits and easy pie fillings. And don't forget refrigerated biscuits, muffin mixes, Bisquick, and the plain or fancy brown 'n serve rolls that are such wonderful busy-day helps.

FOUR-LAYER DINNER

With 40 minutes' notice and these few items from the cupboard shelf, you can have this dinner ready to serve!

1 can (15½ oz.) green
    beans, well drained
8 slices cooked ham
    or 1 can (12 oz.)
    luncheon meat, cut
    into 8 slices
1 can (10½ oz.) cream
    of celery soup

¼ cup mayonnaise
1 tsp. prepared mustard
5 slices process sharp
    American cheese
¼ cup fine dry bread
    crumbs
1 tbsp. butter or
    margarine, melted

Heat oven to 350°. Place beans in 1½-qt. casserole. Top with slices of meat. Mix soup, mayonnaise, and mustard; pour over ham and beans. Top with cheese. Toss bread crumbs with butter; sprinkle over cheese. Bake uncovered 30 min. *6 to 8 servings.*

GOLDEN GATE CASSEROLE

1 pkg. of our noodles
    almondine
2 cups boiling water

1 cup cubed cooked ham
1 avocado

Heat oven to 375°. Empty noodles into 1½-qt. casserole. Sprinkle with seasoned sauce mix. Stir in boiling water and ham. Cover; bake 15 min. Cut avocado in half lengthwise; remove pit and cut avocado into balls with a melon-ball cutter. Gently stir avocado balls into casserole. Cover; bake 5 min. longer. Sprinkle almonds over top before serving. *4 servings.*

SMOKY-RONI

Gay and colorful meal-in-a-dish of macaroni, ham, and broccoli. Serve a salad of crisp red apple and tart grapefruit. Dessert can be date bars—prepared from our mix and baked in the same oven.

1 pkg. of our macaroni
    and Cheddar
1 pkg. (10 oz.) frozen cut
    broccoli, thawed and
    well drained

1 pkg. (3 oz.) smoked
    sliced ham, shredded

Heat oven to 375°. Prepare macaroni and Cheddar as directed on package except—stir in broccoli and ham. Bake covered 20 to 25 min. *4 servings.*

NEW TWIST DISH

½ cup finely chopped
   onion
⅓ cup chopped green
   pepper
1 tbsp. butter or margarine
4 oz. corkscrew-shaped
   macaroni, cooked and
   drained

1 can (12 oz.) pork
   luncheon meat, cubed
1 can (10½ oz.) cream
   of mushroom soup
½ cup catsup
⅓ cup shredded
   Cheddar cheese

Heat oven to 400°. Cook and stir onion and green
pepper in butter until onion is tender. Combine
with remaining ingredients. Pour into 1½-qt. casserole. Cover; bake 30 min., or until bubbly. Garnish with twist of tomato, if desired. *6 servings.*

BAKED SLOPPY JOES

2 cups Bisquick
⅔ cup milk
¼ cup mayonnaise

1 can (15½ oz.) barbecue
  sauce and beef or pork
Paprika

Heat oven to 400°. Grease a square pan, 8x8x2″. Mix Bisquick and milk with fork to a soft dough; beat 20 strokes. Add mayonnaise and mix well. Spread half the mixture into prepared pan. Cover with barbecue sauce and meat mixture. Drop spoonfuls of remaining dough over top. Spread together with a fork. (Top will even out during baking.) Sprinkle with paprika. Bake uncovered 30 to 35 min. Cut into slices, 2x4″. *8 servings.*

TWO-BEAN BAKE

1 can (12 oz.) kidney
  beans, well drained
1 can (1 lb. 1 oz.) Lima
  beans, well drained
½ cup canned spaghetti
  sauce with mushrooms

1 small onion, minced
1 cup shredded Cheddar
  cheese
4 to 6 frankfurters

Heat oven to 375°. Mix beans, spaghetti sauce, onion, and cheese in 1½-qt. casserole. Arrange whole frankfurters on top. Bake uncovered 30 min., or until bean mixture is bubbling and the franks are lightly browned. *4 to 6 servings.*

PIZZA POTATOES

A delicious and colorful "quickie"; pictured here.

1 pkg. of our scalloped
  potatoes
1 can (1 lb.) tomatoes
1½ cups water
¼ tsp. crushed oregano

1 pkg. (4 oz.) sliced
  pepperoni
1 cup shredded
  mozzarella cheese

Heat oven to 400°. Empty potato slices and seasoned sauce mix into baking dish, 9x9x2″. Heat tomatoes, water, and oregano to boiling. Pour over potatoes; stir until well mixed. Arrange pepperoni on top and sprinkle with cheese. Bake uncovered 30 to 35 min. Garnish with hot peppers, if desired. *4 servings.*

CHEESEBURGER CASSEROLE

8 slices day-old bread	1 cup shredded process
Butter	sharp American
½ lb. ground beef	cheese
¼ cup chopped onion	1 egg, beaten
2 tbsp. chopped celery	¾ cup milk
1 tbsp. prepared mustard	½ tsp. salt
½ tsp. salt	Dash pepper
	⅛ tsp. dry mustard

Heat oven to 350°. Toast bread; butter both sides and cut diagonally in half. In skillet, mix ground beef, onion, celery, prepared mustard, and ½ tsp. salt. Cook and stir over medium heat until meat is lightly browned. Arrange toast, hamburger mixture, and cheese in alternate layers in greased square pan, 9x9x2″. Mix remaining ingredients. Pour over layers in pan. Sprinkle with paprika, if desired. Bake uncovered 30 to 35 min. *4 to 6 servings.*

NOODLES NAPOLI

Meat and cheese, noodles, and a vegetable—all are in this dish! Accompany with crisp Italian bread sticks, fruited sundaes for dessert.

1 lb. ground beef	1 cup creamed cottage
1 tsp. salt	cheese
1⅓ cups hot water	1 pkg. (10 oz.) frozen
1 pkg. of our noodles	chopped spinach,
Italiano	thawed and drained
2 eggs, slightly beaten	½ tsp. salt

Heat oven to 375°. Brown ground beef in heavy skillet. Sprinkle with 1 tsp. salt. Mix water with packet of tomato sauce mix from noodles Italiano; stir into meat. Cook and drain noodles as directed on package; fold in eggs, cottage cheese, spinach, ½ tsp. salt, and packet of cheese filling. Place half of the meat sauce in 2-qt. casserole. Cover with noodle mixture; top with remaining meat sauce. Bake uncovered 20 min. *4 servings.*

BEEF 'N CORN CASSEROLE

1 lb. ground beef	1 can (15½ oz.) kidney
4 celery stalks, sliced	beans, drained
2 medium onions,	1 tsp. garlic salt
chopped	Dash pepper
1 can (10½ oz.) tomato	1½ tbsp. Worcestershire
soup	sauce
1 can (1 lb.) cream-style	1 tsp. chili powder
corn	1 pkg. (3¾ oz.) corn
	chips

Heat oven to 375°. Brown ground beef in large heavy skillet. Add celery and onions; cook and stir 3 min. Reduce heat; stir in soup, corn, beans, and seasonings. Pour into 2-qt. casserole. Bake uncovered 20 min. Top with corn chips; bake 10 to 15 min., or until chips are slightly toasted. *8 servings.*

DOUBLE-CHEESE HAMBURGER BAKE

⅓ cup minced onion	½ cup creamed cottage
1 tbsp. minced green	cheese
pepper	1 pkg. (3 oz.) cream
2 tbsp. butter or margarine	cheese, softened
1 lb. ground beef	¼ cup dairy sour cream
1 can (8 oz.) tomato	4 oz. noodles, cooked
sauce	and drained
1 tsp. salt	1 tomato, sliced

Heat oven to 350°. Cook and stir onion and green pepper in butter until onion is tender. Add ground beef; brown. Stir in tomato sauce and salt; simmer 1 min. Remove from heat. Add remaining ingredients except tomato; mix well. Pour into 1½-qt. casserole. Top with tomato slices. Cover; bake 30 min. *4 servings.*

NOODLES FLORENTINE

1 pkg. of our noodles Romanoff	⅓ cup milk
1 pkg. (10 oz.) frozen chopped spinach, cooked and drained	2 tbsp. butter or margarine 4 eggs

Heat oven to 350°. Cook and drain noodles as directed on package. Combine noodles and spinach with milk, butter, and packet of sour cream-cheese sauce mix; stir well. Pour into buttered square pan, 8x8x2". Make four depressions in noodle mixture; break an egg into each. Bake uncovered 20 min., or until eggs are set. *4 servings.*

CAN-CAN CASSEROLE

1 can (11 oz.) Cheddar cheese soup	1 can (9¼ oz.) tuna, drained and flaked
1 can (1 lb.) julienne carrots, drained (reserve ⅓ cup liquid)	1 can (15 oz.) macaroni and cheese
¾ tsp. crushed rosemary	¼ cup minced parsley
¼ tsp. pepper	1 can (3½ oz.) French fried onion rings

Heat oven to 375°. Mix soup with reserved liquid from carrots. Stir in rosemary and pepper. Spread tuna in oblong baking dish, 11½x7½x1½". Layer with macaroni and cheese, carrots, and parsley. Pour cheese soup mixture over layers. Bake uncovered 30 to 35 min., or until bubbly. Top with onion rings and bake 5 min. longer. *6 to 8 servings.*

TUNA-SPINACH BAKE

¼ cup butter or margarine	1 tbsp. lemon juice
¼ cup Gold Medal Flour (regular or Wondra)	1 can (6½ oz.) tuna, drained and flaked
1 tsp. salt	2 lb. fresh spinach, chopped, or 2 pkg. (10 oz. each) frozen chopped spinach, cooked and drained
¼ tsp. pepper	
¼ tsp. dry mustard	
⅛ tsp. onion salt	
2 cups milk	
½ cup mayonnaise	1 cup croutons

Heat oven to 350°. Melt butter in saucepan. Blend in flour and seasonings. Cook over low heat, stirring until mixture is smooth and bubbly. Remove from heat. Stir in milk. Heat to boiling, stirring constantly. Boil 1 min. Blend in mayonnaise and lemon juice. Spread tuna in oblong baking dish, 10x6x1½". Top with half the sauce; mix remaining sauce with spinach. Pour over tuna. Sprinkle with croutons. Bake uncovered 25 to 30 min. *6 servings.*

MOCK OYSTER CASSEROLE

1 can (10½ oz.) chicken
    with rice soup
1 can (10½ oz.) cream of
    mushroom soup
2 cans (6½ oz. each)
    tuna, well drained and
    broken into chunks
1 can (3 oz.) sliced
    mushrooms, drained

1 jar (2 oz.) pimiento,
    cut up
½ cup chopped green
    pepper
1 small onion, chopped
¼ tsp. pepper
¼ cup chopped toasted
    almonds
3 cups oyster crackers
6 tomato slices

Heat oven to 350°. In a medium bowl, mix the soups until well blended. Stir in remaining ingredients except tomato slices. Pour into greased oblong baking dish, 11½x7½x1½". Bake uncovered 30 to 35 min. Top with tomato slices. Garnish with parsley, if desired. *6 to 8 servings.*

CURRIED TUNA CASSEROLE

Isn't it hard to believe that this company-pretty dinner, pictured above, can be prepared so quickly?

2 tbsp. butter or margarine
1½ tsp. curry powder
1 can (10½ oz.) cream
    of mushroom soup
¾ cup milk

2 cans (6½ oz. each)
    tuna, drained
2½ cups cooked rice
1 can (8 oz.) onions,
    drained and halved
Curry Condiments

Heat oven to 350°. Brown butter and curry powder in small skillet. Mix with soup, milk, tuna, rice, and onions. Pour into 2-qt. casserole. Bake uncovered 30 min. Quickly top with a design of Curry Condiments—sieved hard-cooked egg yolks, chopped peanuts, plumped currants, crabapple jelly, sliced green onions, and crumbled bacon. *6 servings.*

SPEEDY SALMON GOURMET

1 pkg. of our noodles
   Romanoff
⅔ cup milk
1 can (7¾ oz.) salmon,
   drained and flaked

½ cup creamed cottage
   cheese
1 tbsp. chopped chives,
   if desired

Heat oven to 350°. Prepare noodles Romanoff as directed on package except—use ⅔ cup milk. Stir in remaining ingredients. Pour into 1-qt. casserole. Cover and bake 15 to 20 min. *4 servings.*

SALMON AND PASTA

½ cup chopped onion
¼ cup butter or margarine
2 tbsp. flour
1 can (1 lb.) salmon,
   drained (reserve liquid)
1¾ cups milk
½ tsp. salt

⅛ tsp. paprika
1 tbsp. lemon juice
¼ cup minced parsley
5 oz. elbow macaroni,
   cooked and drained
2 cups shredded Cheddar
   cheese

Heat oven to 375°. Cook and stir onion in butter until tender. Remove from heat. Blend in flour. Cook over low heat, stirring until mixture is bubbly. Remove from heat. Stir in reserved liquid from salmon and the milk. Heat to boiling, stirring constantly. Boil 1 min. Remove from heat. Stir in salt, paprika, lemon juice, and parsley. Break salmon into bite-size pieces. Layer macaroni, salmon, and ¾ of the cheese in 2-qt. casserole. Pour sauce over layers; sprinkle with remaining cheese. Bake uncovered 20 to 25 min., or until sauce is bubbly and cheese is melted. *6 to 8 servings.*

DIXIE CRAB BAKE

¼ cup butter or margarine
2 tbsp. flour
1 cup light cream
1 tsp. prepared mustard
½ tsp. salt
¼ tsp. pepper
¼ tsp. mace
1 tbsp. lemon juice
1 can (1 lb.) sliced carrots,
   drained

2 cans (7½ oz. each)
   crabmeat, drained
   and cartilage removed
2 hard-cooked eggs,
   finely chopped
2 cups soft bread crumbs
2 tbsp. butter, melted
Lemon wedges

Heat oven to 350°. Melt butter in heavy saucepan; stir in flour. Cook over low heat, stirring until mixture is smooth and bubbly. Remove from heat. Stir in cream; heat to boiling, stirring constantly. Boil 1 min. Gently fold in seasonings, carrots, crabmeat, and eggs. Pour mixture into 1½-qt. casserole. Toss bread crumbs with butter; sprinkle over top. Bake uncovered 45 min., or until bubbly. Serve with lemon wedges. *4 to 6 servings.*

SIMPLE-SAUCY FISH BAKE

1 pkg. (1 lb.) frozen ocean
   perch fillets
½ tsp. salt
⅛ tsp. pepper
1 tbsp. butter
1 can (1 lb. 3 oz.)
   asparagus spears,
   drained

1 pkg. (1¾ oz.) Hollandaise
   sauce mix
Paprika
1 can (3½ oz.) French
   fried onion rings

Thaw fillets just until they can be separated. Heat oven to 475°. If desired, skin fillets. Sprinkle both sides of fillets with salt; place at ends of oblong baking dish, 11½x7½x1½″, leaving a space in center of dish. Sprinkle fillets with pepper and dot with butter. Bake uncovered 15 minutes. Prepare Hollandaise sauce mix as directed on package. Remove fish from oven. Place asparagus spears in center of dish; pour heated Hollandaise sauce over asparagus. Sprinkle sauce with paprika. Bake uncovered 5 minutes, or until fish is done. Sprinkle onion rings over the fish. Bake 2 minutes longer, or until onion rings are golden brown. *3 to 4 servings.*

Skillet Quick

When the situation calls for super speed, get out your trusty skillet or electric frypan and stir up one of these delectable, easy one-dish dinners. Serve right from the skillet, if you like; many skillets are so attractive you can proudly place them on the table to keep food hot and to simplify serving.

Among these recipes you'll find hamburger specialties that add new interest to family meals, scrambled egg variations to brighten workday menus at little cost, and many other "quickie" meals you can speed to a tasty finish with the help of canned or packaged foods.

GOURMET CHICKEN AND NOODLES ALMONDINE

1 pkg. of our noodles almondine	½ cup dairy sour cream
1 cup diced cooked chicken or turkey	1 tbsp. sherry
	½ tsp. grated lemon peel

Prepare noodles almondine as directed on package for range-top method. Stir in remaining ingredients; heat through. *4 servings.*

HAM 'N CABBAGE QUICKIE

1 tbsp. butter or margarine	1 tsp. caraway seed
1 small head cabbage (about 1½ lb.), shredded	¼ tsp. chili pepper or chili powder
1 cup cut-up cooked ham	1 can (1 lb.) small potatoes, drained
1 tsp. salt	

Melt butter in heavy skillet. Add cabbage, ham, and seasonings. Cover tightly. Steam 5 min., stirring several times. Add potatoes; heat through. *4 to 6 servings.*

FRANKS WITH SWEET-SOUR CABBAGE

Old-fashioned flavor in a minimum of minutes! This hearty dish is pictured here.

8 cups shredded cabbage	2 tsp. caraway seed
¼ cup butter or margarine	2 tsp. celery salt
⅓ cup vinegar	1 tsp. salt
¼ cup brown sugar (packed)	8 frankfurters

In heavy skillet, cook and stir cabbage in butter until lightly browned. Mix remaining ingredients except frankfurters; stir into cabbage. Place frankfurters on top. Cover tightly; cook over low heat 8 min. Garnish with celery leaves, if desired. *4 servings.*

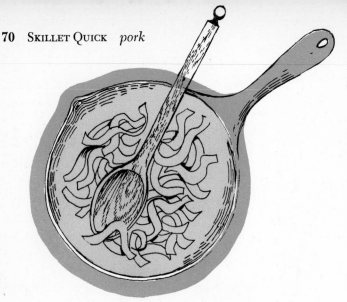

MEXICAN MEDLEY

1 lb. bulk pork sausage	1 can (1 lb.) tomatoes
1 cup finely chopped onion	1 cup dairy sour cream
1 cup finely chopped green pepper	¾ cup water
	1 tbsp. sugar
7 or 8 oz. uncooked wide noodles	2 tsp. salt
	1 to 2 tsp. chili powder

In heavy skillet, cook and stir sausage, onion, and green pepper until meat is browned and onion is tender. Drain off excess fat. Stir in remaining ingredients. Cover; simmer 30 min., or until noodles are tender. (Add more water, if necessary.) Garnish with parsley, if desired. *4 to 6 servings.*

SMOKY MOUNTAIN SKILLET BEANS

Lima beans and smoked sausages in a delightful sour cream sauce. Pass rye bread, a relish plate of sliced fresh tomatoes.

1 pkg. (8 oz.) smoked pork sausage links, cut in half	1 tbsp. molasses
	½ tsp. salt
	½ tsp. dry mustard
1 cup dairy sour cream	2 cans (1 lb. each) Lima beans, drained
2 tbsp. brown sugar	
1 tbsp. butter or margarine	Sliced pimiento-stuffed olives

Cook sausages in skillet as directed on package; drain off excess fat. Stir in sour cream, brown sugar, butter, molasses, salt, and dry mustard. Heat, stirring constantly, over low heat until sauce is smooth. Do not boil. Add beans and heat through. Serve garnished with sliced olives. *4 to 6 servings.*

SESAME-SOY PORK

1 lb. lean pork, cut into thin strips (about ⅛″ thick)	1 cup thinly sliced celery
	1 pkg. (10 oz.) frozen French-style green beans, thawed
2 tbsp. salad oil	
½ tsp. salt	¼ cup finely chopped onion
¼ tsp. pepper	
½ cup water	3 tbsp. soy sauce
5 oz. noodles, cooked and drained	¼ cup water
	Toasted sesame seed*

Brown pork in hot oil in large heavy skillet; season with salt and pepper. Remove from heat; pour in ½ cup water. Cover and simmer until meat is tender, about 30 min. (Add more water, if necessary.) Stir in remaining ingredients except sesame seed. Cover; cook over medium heat about 5 min. longer, or until celery and beans are as tender as you like. Sprinkle toasted sesame seed over each serving. *6 to 8 servings.*

*To toast sesame seed, place in ungreased skillet over medium heat, stirring frequently, until delicately browned.

VEAL DI NAPOLI

Quick and colorful—pictured above.

1½ lb. veal cutlets	1 can (1 lb.) whole
2 tbsp. salad oil	onions, drained
1 tsp. salt	1 can (6 oz.) sliced
1 can (1 lb.) tomatoes	mushrooms, drained
1 pkg. (1½ oz.) spaghetti	(reserve ¼ cup liquid)
sauce mix with	1 can (1 lb.) peas and
mushrooms	carrots, drained
⅓ cup sherry	

Pound cutlets ¼″ thick with wooden mallet; cut into serving-size pieces. In large skillet, brown veal quickly in hot oil. Season meat with salt. In same skillet, combine tomatoes, spaghetti sauce mix, and sherry. Heat to boiling; cover and simmer 10 minutes, stirring occasionally. Add onions, mushrooms (with reserved liquid), and peas and carrots. Cover and simmer 10 minutes. Garnish with parsley, if desired. *6 servings.*

CORNED BEEF HASH SUPREME

Delicious teamed with pineapple-cabbage slaw and pumpernickel bread.

2 cloves garlic, minced	2 cans (1 lb. each) corned
½ cup chopped onion	beef hash, crumbled
1 can (6 oz.) sliced mush-	⅔ cup dairy sour cream
rooms, drained	¼ cup minced parsley
3 to 4 tbsp. butter or	4 medium tomatoes,
margarine	sliced ¼″ thick
	Grated Parmesan cheese

In large skillet, cook and stir garlic, onion, and mushrooms in butter until onion is tender. Add hash; brown well, scraping bottom of pan frequently. (If necessary, thin sour cream with water until of pouring consistency.) Combine sour cream and parsley; stir into hash mixture. Top with tomato slices. Cover; cook over medium heat about 5 min., or until tomatoes are hot. Sprinkle with cheese. *4 to 6 servings.*

CHEESEBURGERS IN VEGETABLE SAUCE

8 thin hamburger patties	1 can (12 oz.) whole
Salt and pepper	kernel corn with
4 slices process American	peppers, drained
cheese	2 tbsp. chili sauce
1 can (10½ oz.) vegetable	
soup	

In large heavy skillet, brown patties well on both sides; season lightly with salt and pepper. Drain off excess fat. Place cheese slices on four of the meat patties; top with remaining patties, making 4 hamburger-cheese stacks. Combine soup, corn, and chili sauce. Pour over and around meat. Cover and simmer 10 min., stirring occasionally. *4 servings.*

CREAMY BEEF-TOMATO SKILLET

1 lb. ground beef	1 medium green pepper,
½ lb. ground pork	diced
1 can (1 lb. 13 oz.)	1 clove garlic, minced
tomatoes	1 jar (2 oz.) pimiento,
1 can (8 oz.) tomato	cut up
sauce	2 tbsp. sugar
7 or 8 oz. uncooked	2 tsp. chili powder
elbow macaroni	2 tsp. salt
1 large onion, chopped	1 cup dairy sour cream

Brown meat in large skillet. Drain off all the fat as it collects. Stir in remaining ingredients except sour cream. Heat to boiling. Cover and simmer 20 min., or until macaroni is tender; stir frequently. Stir in sour cream; heat through but do not boil. *6 servings.*

CALYPSO SKILLET

Ground beef, corn, and saucy noodles—a meal-in-one the whole family will love!

1 lb. ground beef	5 oz. uncooked narrow
½ cup chopped onion	noodles
1 can (8 oz.) whole kernel	1 tsp. crushed oregano
corn, drained (reserve	½ tsp. salt
liquid)	¼ tsp. pepper
1 can (8 oz.) tomato	1 cup shredded process
sauce	sharp American
¼ cup halved pitted	cheese
ripe olives	

In large skillet, cook and stir meat and onion until meat is browned and onion is tender. Drain off fat. Add enough water to reserved corn liquid to make 2 cups. Stir liquid and remaining ingredients into the meat mixture. Simmer uncovered, stirring occasionally, 15 to 20 min., or until of desired consistency. *4 to 6 servings.*

MINUTE-SAVER GOULASH

1 lb. ground beef	1 tbsp. salad oil
1 small onion, minced	1 pkg. of our noodles
1 cup diced celery	Italiano
	2⅓ cups hot water

In large skillet, cook and stir ground beef, the onion, and celery in hot oil until meat is browned and onion is tender. Stir in tomato sauce mix, cheese mix, and noodles from package. Add water; heat to boiling. Cover; reduce heat and simmer 20 min., stirring occasionally. *4 to 6 servings.*

QUICKIE CHERRY BROWNIES

For dessert, here's another time-saver. Just prepare 1 package of our fudge brownie mix as directed on package except—add ¼ cup well-drained chopped maraschino cherries to the batter. A flavor favorite.

MAHARAJA'S DELIGHT

¾ cup finely chopped
   onion
¾ tsp. curry powder
¼ cup butter or margarine
6 eggs
⅓ cup milk or light cream
¾ tsp. salt
¼ tsp. pepper

1½ cups cooked rice
1 pkg. (10 oz.) frozen
   asparagus cuts, cooked
   and drained
2 slices bacon, crisply
   fried and crumbled, or
1 tbsp. chopped
   chutney

Cook and stir onion and curry powder in butter until onion is tender. Combine eggs, milk, salt, and pepper; beat with fork until blended. Stir in rice and asparagus; add mixture to skillet. Cook over low heat. When mixture begins to set at bottom and sides, lift cooked portions with spatula and turn gently to cook evenly. (Eggs should still be moist and glossy.) Top with bacon or chutney. *4 servings.*

FRITTATA

Platter partner—toasted English muffins spread with sparkling currant jelly.

9 eggs
2 tbsp. milk
½ tsp. salt
½ cup grated Parmesan
   cheese
2 cups finely chopped
   fresh spinach

½ cup minced parsley
½ cup finely chopped
   onion
1 clove garlic, minced
2 tbsp. salad oil

Beat eggs slightly. Mix in remaining ingredients except oil. Heat oil in heavy medium skillet. Pour in the egg mixture; cook over low heat. When mixture begins to set at bottom and sides, lift cooked portions with spatula and turn gently to cook evenly. (Eggs should still be moist and glossy.) Serve on heated platter. *6 to 8 servings.*

SCRAMBLED EGGS CORONADO

An ideal Sunday supper; pictured here.

9 eggs
½ cup light cream
1¼ tsp. salt
¼ tsp. pepper

1 avocado, peeled and
   cubed (about 1 cup)
¼ lb. sliced bacon
3 to 4 chilled tomatoes,
   sliced, or cherry
   tomatoes

Beat eggs and cream with fork. Add salt, pepper, and avocado. Fry bacon until crisp; drain on paper towels. Drain all but 3 tbsp. bacon fat from skillet; heat. Pour in egg mixture; cook over low heat. When mixture starts to set at bottom and sides, lift cooked portions with spatula and turn gently to cook evenly. Crumble bacon and sprinkle over eggs. Cook about 5 min. longer. (Eggs should still be moist and glossy.) Serve with sliced tomatoes. *6 to 8 servings.*

WEST COAST CAULIFLOWER

Complete the meal with hot cheese biscuits, Cucumber Relish Mold (p. 150). Pictured at right.

1 pkg. (10 oz.) frozen cauliflower	**¼ cup milk**
1 pkg. (10 oz.) frozen green peas	**¼ tsp. salt**
1 can (10½ oz.) frozen cream of shrimp soup	**⅛ tsp. pepper**
	2 cups cleaned cooked or canned shrimp
	Toasted almonds

Cook cauliflower and peas in ½ to 1″ boiling salted water just until tender, about 3 to 5 min.; drain. Heat soup, milk, salt, and pepper over low heat, stirring constantly. Stir in cauliflower, peas, and shrimp; heat through. Pour into serving dish and sprinkle with toasted almonds. Garnish with lemon slices and parsley, if desired. *4 servings.*

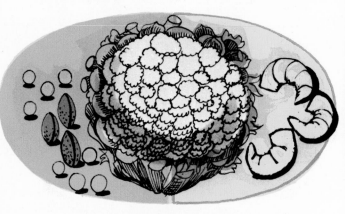

TUNA PILAF

1 small onion, thinly sliced	**3 cups cooked rice (cooked without salt)**
½ cup diagonally sliced celery	**2 cans (6½ oz. each) tuna, drained**
1 tbsp. salad oil	**1 can (5 oz.) water chestnuts, sliced paper-thin**
1 pkg. (10 oz.) frozen mixed vegetables	**¼ cup soy sauce**
½ cup water	

In large heavy skillet, cook and stir onion and celery in hot oil until onion is tender. Add vegetables and water; heat just to boiling. Cover tightly and simmer 10 min., or until vegetables are tender. Add remaining ingredients; stir gently until well mixed. Heat through. *6 to 8 servings.*

For meals in mere minutes, the broiler can be a cook's best friend! Preparation is simple; the cooking's a cinch. And your whole dinner comes sizzling hot from the broiler with scarcely a pot or a pan to wash.

Thick, juicy lamb chops with crusty herbed bread, seafood and vegetable kabobs, glazed meat and sweet potatoes–all done to a golden turn and timed for split-second serving. You will find these and more dinners-from-the-broiler in this chapter.

BALI HAI BANQUET
Meat Stack-ups
Carameled Sweet Potatoes 'n Pineapple

**1 can (12 oz.) pork
luncheon meat
Prepared mustard
1 can (1 lb. 1 oz.) sweet
potatoes, drained
1 can (8½ oz.) pineapple
slices, drained and
halved (reserve 2 tbsp.
syrup)**

**½ cup brown sugar
(packed)
2 tbsp. butter or
margarine
⅛ tsp. salt
2 tbsp. flaked coconut**

Cut luncheon meat into 8 slices. Spread 4 slices with mustard; cover with remaining slices, making 4 sandwiches. Arrange meat on broiler rack. Form an 8″ square pan from heavy-duty aluminum foil; place on broiler rack. Alternate sweet potatoes and pineapple halves in pan. Mix brown sugar, butter, reserved pineapple syrup, and salt; pour over potatoes and pineapple slices. Set oven control at "broil." Broil 4 or 5″ from source of heat 4 min., or until meat begins to brown. Turn meat; broil an additional 4 or 5 min., or until potatoes are heated through. Sprinkle coconut over potatoes and pineapple; broil 1 min. longer, or until coconut is lightly toasted. *4 servings.*

COOK'S TIPS FOR BROILING

• Place the broiler rack so that the top of the food is the correct distance from source of heat as directed in each recipe.

• Broil with door closed in gas range. In most electric ranges, broil with door ajar —check manufacturer's directions.

• When broiling vegetables and lean fish and meat —grease broiler rack so food won't stick.

• Before broiling cuts of meat, slash fat edge at 1-inch intervals to prevent meat from curling. Always turn meat with tongs or with a fork inserted in fat edge. No loss of good meat juices this way!

• Broiled foods cool more quickly than roasted or baked ones. For a sizzling hot broiler meal, serve immediately on heated plates.

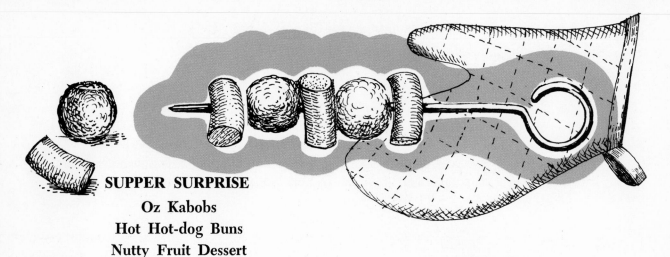

SUPPER SURPRISE

Oz Kabobs
Hot Hot-dog Buns
Nutty Fruit Dessert

1 can (1 lb. 14 oz.) fruit
   cocktail, drained
   (reserve 2 tbsp. syrup)
1 orange, peeled and
   sectioned
¼ cup brown sugar
   (packed)
2 tbsp. chopped walnuts
   or pecans
1 tsp. grated orange peel
¼ tsp. nutmeg
½ lb. ground beef
½ cup Wheaties
1 egg

1 tbsp. milk
1 tbsp. instant minced
   onion
½ tsp. seasoned salt
⅛ tsp. pepper
4 cubes Cheddar cheese,
   ¾" each
4 cubes dill pickle, ¾"
   each
4 frankfurters, cut into
   thirds
4 frankfurter buns,
   buttered

Combine fruit cocktail and orange sections; divide among 4 individual aluminum foil tart pans. Mix brown sugar, nuts, orange peel, nutmeg, and reserved fruit cocktail syrup. Spoon over fruit. Mix ground beef, Wheaties, egg, milk, onion, and seasonings. Shape into 8 balls, forming each around 1 cube of cheese or pickle. On each of 4 skewers, alternate 3 pieces of frankfurter with 2 meatballs. Wrap buns in heavy-duty aluminum foil. Arrange meat kabobs and foil package on broiler rack. Set oven control at "broil." Broil 4" from source of heat 4 min. Turn kabobs and foil package; place foil tart pans on rack. Continue broiling 4 min., or until meatballs are done. To serve, slip meat off skewers into buns. *4 servings.*

KABOB DINNER

Kabobs of Lemon-buttered Scallops,
Parmesan Potatoes,
Pineapple, Mushrooms, Tomatoes,
Green Pepper

1 lb. fresh or frozen
   scallops
¼ cup butter or
   margarine, melted
1 tbsp. lemon juice
½ tsp. paprika
½ tsp. salt
⅛ tsp. pepper
1 can (1 lb.) potatoes,
   drained

Soft butter
Grated Parmesan cheese
1 can (13½ oz.) pine-
   apple chunks, drained
1 can (4 oz.) button
   mushrooms, drained
2 tomatoes, cut into
   eighths
1 green pepper, cut into
   1" pieces

If using frozen scallops, thaw in the refrigerator. Wash scallops and remove any shell particles. Mix melted butter with lemon juice, paprika, salt, and pepper. Dip scallops into butter mixture. Brush potatoes with soft butter and sprinkle with Parmesan cheese. On long metal skewers, alternate scallops, potatoes, pineapple chunks, mushrooms, tomato wedges, and green pepper pieces. Set oven control at "broil." Place kabobs on greased broiler rack and broil 3 to 5" from source of heat 3 to 4 min.; turn and broil 3 to 5 min. longer. Serve with lemon wedges, if desired. *4 servings.*

LAMB GRILL DELUXE
Broiled Lamb Chops
Lemon-glazed Carrots and Artichokes
Rosemary Bread

6 to 8 carrots	1 small loaf French
4 canned whole	bread or 4 hard-
artichoke hearts	crusted rolls
⅓ cup brown sugar	Soft butter
(packed)	Crushed rosemary
2 tbsp. soft butter	4 loin lamb chops, 1″
1 tsp. grated lemon peel	thick
1 tsp. lemon juice	Salt and pepper

Cut carrots into 3 or 4″ lengths. Cook in ½ to 1″ boiling salted water until tender; drain. Place carrots and artichoke hearts in 9″ foil pan (can be made from heavy-duty aluminum foil). Mix brown sugar, 2 tbsp. butter, the lemon peel, and lemon juice; spoon over carrots and artichoke hearts. Cut French bread into 1″ slices, or slice rolls in half. Spread with butter and sprinkle with rosemary.

Slash edges of chops in several places to prevent curling; place on broiler rack. Set oven control at "broil." Broil chops 3 to 4″ from source of heat 6 min. for medium done meat, 7 min. for well done. Season chops with salt and pepper; turn. Place foil pan on broiler rack. Broil 6 or 7 min., as desired. During the last 3 min. place bread buttered side up on rack. Season chops; serve meal on heated platter or plate. Garnish meat with cherry tomatoes, if desired. *4 servings.*

SEA AND GARDEN GRILL
Broiler-browned Fish Sticks
Parmesan Zucchini
Dilled Tomato Halves

4 small or 2 medium zucchini squash	Butter
	¼ tsp. dill weed
Soft butter	Salt and pepper
Salt and pepper	1 pkg. (8 oz.) frozen fish sticks
Grated Parmesan cheese	
2 tomatoes, peeled and sliced in half	Lemon wedges

Cut zucchini in half lengthwise; cook in boiling salted water until almost tender, about 5 min.; drain well. Place cut side up on greased broiler rack. Brush with soft butter; sprinkle with salt and pepper and the Parmesan cheese. Arrange the tomato halves on rack; dot lightly with butter; sprinkle with dill weed and lightly season with salt and pepper. Place frozen fish sticks on rack. Set oven control at "broil." Broil 4" from source of heat 5 min., or until vegetables and fish sticks are heated through. Serve on warm platter garnished with lemon wedges. *4 servings.*

BROILED SALMON SPECIAL
Lemon-buttered Salmon Steaks
Hashed Brown Potatoes
Chutney Peaches

¼ cup lemon juice	Seasoned salt
2 tsp. crushed marjoram	Pepper
2 tsp. onion salt	4 salmon steaks, 1" thick
1 pkg. (12 oz.) frozen hashed brown potatoes	1 can (1 lb.) peach halves, drained
Melted butter	Chopped chutney

Mix the lemon juice, marjoram, and onion salt; set aside. Grease broiler rack. Place frozen potato patties on rack; brush with melted butter and sprinkle lightly with seasoned salt and pepper. Set oven control at "broil." Broil 4 to 5" from source of heat 5 min. Brush patties again with melted butter. Place salmon on rack; drizzle with melted butter and spoon half of the lemon mixture over the fish. Broil fish and potatoes 4 to 5 min. Turn salmon and potatoes over. Brush potatoes with melted butter and sprinkle with seasoned salt and pepper. Drizzle salmon with melted butter and season lightly with pepper. Spoon remaining lemon mixture over the salmon.

Place peach halves on broiler rack; spoon 1 tsp. chopped chutney into center of each peach. Broil potatoes, fish, and peaches 4 min., or until fish flakes easily with a fork and potatoes are golden brown. Serve on a heated platter. *4 servings.*

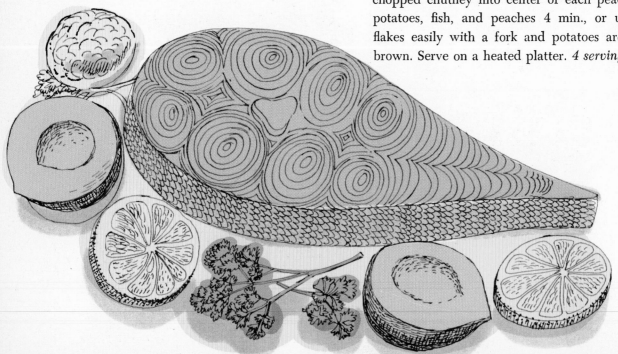

Hearty and Homestyle

These one-dish dinners are down-to-earth, everyday meals—real home cooking. Pot roasts, meat pies, and baked beans are the kind of robust family fare Americans everywhere enjoy year after year.

Looking through these homespun recipes, you will find faithful standbys that will jog your memory with a nostalgic wish to enjoy them soon again. Others, perhaps new to you, may soon be on your family's list of favorite foods. All are old-fashioned good eating—not fancy, but fully fine enough to share with guests.

Served with a slice of homemade bread, hot baking powder biscuits or golden corn bread, they warm the heart and satisfy the appetite in familiar, wholesome ways.

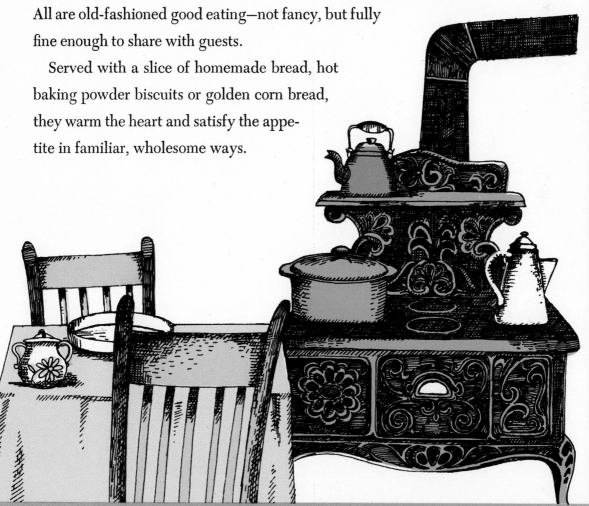

Meat Pies—*Country kitchen fare with a long and noble history.*

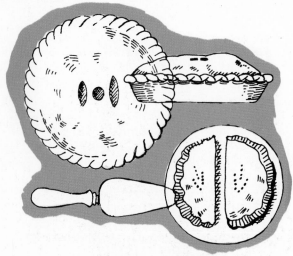

SALMON PIE

2 sticks of our pie crust mix	2 tbsp. minced parsley
2 eggs, beaten	¾ tsp. crushed basil
½ cup milk	¼ tsp. salt
1 tbsp. butter or margarine, melted	1 can (1 lb.) salmon, drained
¼ cup chopped onion	Egg Sauce (below)

Heat oven to 425°. Prepare pastry for 9″ Two-crust Pie as directed on inside wrapper. Mix eggs, milk, butter, onion, parsley, basil, and salt. Break salmon into pieces, removing bones and skin. Stir salmon into egg mixture. Pour into pastry-lined pie pan. Cover with top crust which has slits cut in it. Seal and flute. Cover crust edge with 1½″ strip aluminum foil to prevent excessive browning. Bake 35 to 40 min. Serve hot with Egg Sauce. *6 servings.*

EGG SAUCE

¼ cup butter or margarine	¼ tsp. pepper
¼ cup Gold Medal Flour (regular or Wondra)	2 cups milk
½ tsp. salt	4 hard-cooked eggs, diced

Melt butter over low heat. Blend in flour, salt, and pepper. Cook over low heat, stirring until mixture is smooth and bubbly. Remove from heat. Stir in milk. Heat to boiling, stirring constantly. Boil 1 min. Carefully stir in eggs; heat. Season to taste.

TUNA CONFETTI PIE

Cheese Pastry (p. 83)	1 can (10½ oz.) cream of asparagus soup
1 pkg. (10 oz.) frozen mixed vegetables	⅔ cup milk
1 can (10½ oz.) cream of celery soup	1 can (9¼ oz.) tuna, drained
	¼ cup minced onion

Heat oven to 425°. Roll out ⅔ of pastry ⅛″ thick; trim to 13″ square. Fit pastry into baking dish, 8x8x2″, extending pastry ½″ beyond edges of pan. Roll out remaining pastry; trim to 9″ square. Cook vegetables as directed on package except—use unsalted water; drain. Combine soups and milk; fold in cooked vegetables, tuna, and onion. Pour into pastry-lined pan. Cover with top square of pastry. Turn edges of bottom crust over edges of top crust. Press lightly against side of pan; flute edges if desired. Cut 3 or 4 slits near center to allow steam to escape. Bake 25 to 30 min., or until crust is golden brown. *6 servings.*

SAUCY TURNOVERS

1 pkg. (10 oz.) frozen mixed vegetables	Celery Seed Pastry (p. 83)
2 tbsp. grated onion	Egg and Cheese Sauce (below)

Heat oven to 425°. Cook frozen vegetables as directed on package, adding onion to water; drain well. Divide pastry into 6 equal parts. Roll out each ⅛″ thick; trim to a 6″ circle; arrange on baking sheet. Place a scant ⅓ cup of cooled vegetables on each circle. Moisten edges of pastry; fold into a half moon. Seal edges with tines of fork; prick tops. Bake 15 to 20 min., or until nicely browned. Serve with Egg and Cheese Sauce. *Makes 6 turnovers.*

EGG AND CHEESE SAUCE

Combine 1 can (11 oz.) Cheddar cheese soup, ⅓ cup milk, and 1 tbsp. parsley flakes; cook over low heat, stirring occasionally. Add 3 cut-up hard-cooked eggs; heat through.

CHICKEN DINNER PIE

The all-time favorite, pictured below.

Two-crust Pastry (p. 83)	2 cups cubed cooked
2 tbsp. butter or margarine	chicken
2 tbsp. flour	1 can (1 lb.) peas and
1 tsp. salt	carrots, drained, or
⅛ tsp. pepper	1 pkg. (10 oz.) frozen
⅛ tsp. ground thyme	peas and carrots,
½ cup chicken broth	cooked and drained
½ cup light cream	1 can (8 oz.) small whole
	onions, drained

Heat oven to 425°. Roll out ⅔ of the pastry ⅛" thick. Fit into 9" pie pan. Trim pastry, leaving 1" edge. Roll out remaining pastry ⅛" thick into rectangle, about 10x6"; cut into 12 strips, ½" wide.

Melt butter over low heat. Blend in flour, salt, pepper, thyme. Cook over low heat, stirring until mixture is smooth and bubbly. Remove from heat. Stir in chicken broth and cream. Heat to boiling, stirring constantly. Boil 1 min. Stir in chicken and vegetables. Pour into pastry-lined pie pan. Place 7 strips of pastry across filling; arrange remaining strips crisscross fashion to make a lattice-type top. Trim; turn edge of bottom crust over strips. Seal and flute. Bake 35 to 40 min., or until nicely browned. *6 servings.*

LATTICE-TOPPED MEATBALL BAKE

1½ cups soft bread cubes	½ cup green pepper
⅓ cup milk	strips
1 lb. ground beef	½ cup chopped celery
½ cup finely chopped	½ cup chopped onion
onion	½ clove garlic, minced
1¼ tsp. salt	1 can (1 lb.) tomatoes
⅛ tsp. thyme	One-crust Pastry (p. 83)

Soak bread cubes in milk; mix in meat, ½ cup onion, the salt, and thyme. Form into twenty-five to thirty ½" balls and brown in small amount of hot fat. Remove meatballs. Add green pepper, celery, ½ cup onion, and garlic; cook and stir until tender. Drain excess fat from skillet. Add tomatoes and meatballs; heat through. Pour into baking dish, 11½x7½x1½".

Heat oven to 425°. Roll pastry ⅛" thick; cut into 1" strips. Arrange crisscross over top of casserole, trimming strips at edge of dish. Place another strip of pastry around inside edge of dish; lightly press to seal. Bake 35 to 40 min., or until pastry is nicely browned. *6 to 8 servings.*

CHICKEN-SAUSAGE PIES

These little pies, topped with Chicken Littles in the picture below, hold a surprise of hot fruit. Delicious!

½ lb. bulk pork sausage
1 can (3 oz.) chopped mushrooms, drained (reserve ¼ cup liquid)
¼ cup butter or margarine
¼ cup Gold Medal Flour (regular or Wondra)
¼ tsp. salt
2 cups chicken broth*
1 cup light cream
1 can (1 lb. 14 oz.) peach halves, well drained
2 cups cut-up cooked chicken
Two-crust Pastry (p. 83)

Shape pork sausage into 1″ balls. Brown on all sides in medium skillet; remove and drain on paper towels. Drain fat from skillet. In same skillet, cook and stir mushrooms in melted butter for 5 min. Remove from heat. Stir in flour and salt. Cook over low heat, stirring until mixture is bubbly. Remove from heat. Stir in chicken broth, cream, and reserved mushroom liquid. Heat to boiling, stirring constantly. Boil 1 min. Place a peach half in each of six 1½-cup individual casseroles; top with chicken and sausage balls. Pour cream sauce over meat.

Heat oven to 425°. Roll out half of pastry ⅛″ thick. Cut 3 circles, allowing pastry to be 2″ larger in diameter than top of filled casseroles. Place each circle on a casserole. Fold pastry under, making it even with edge of dish; flute. Cut slits near center. Repeat with remaining pastry. Place casseroles on baking sheet; lay piece of aluminum foil over tops. Bake 20 min. Remove foil and bake 10 min. longer, or until crust is nicely browned. If desired, stand a Chicken Little (right) upright in center of each baked crust; surround with garnish of parsley or sliced pimiento. *6 servings.*

*Chicken broth may be made by dissolving 2 chicken bouillon cubes in 2 cups boiling water, or use 1 can (13¾ oz.) chicken broth.

CHICKEN LITTLES

To prepare chickens as shown here, roll out remaining pieces of pastry about ¼″ thick. Cut with a 2½″ chicken-shaped cookie cutter. Or with a knife, trace around a cardboard pattern. Place chicken cutouts on ungreased baking sheet. Insert a wooden pick halfway into each chicken. Bake in same oven with Chicken-Sausage Pies for 15 to 20 min., or until nicely browned.

STANDARD PASTRY

One-crust Pastry
1 cup Gold Medal Flour*
  (regular or Wondra)
½ tsp. salt
⅓ cup plus 1 tbsp.
  shortening or ⅓ cup
  lard
2 tbsp. water

Two-crust Pastry
2 cups Gold Medal Flour*
  (regular or Wondra)
1 tsp. salt
⅔ cup plus 2 tbsp.
  shortening or ⅔ cup
  lard
4 tbsp. water

Mix flour and salt. Cut in shortening thoroughly. *Sprinkle* water gradually over mixture, a tbsp. at a time, tossing lightly with a fork after each addition. (If dough appears dry, a few drops of water may be added.) Gather dough into a ball. On a lightly floured cloth-covered board, roll out dough as directed in the meat pie recipe.

*If using Gold Medal Self-Rising Flour, omit salt.

CHEESE PASTRY

Prepare Two-crust Pastry as directed above except —decrease salt to ½ tsp., then mix in 1 cup shredded Cheddar cheese after cutting in the shortening.

CELERY SEED PASTRY

Prepare Two-crust Pastry as directed above except —mix 1 tsp. celery seed into dry ingredients.

Betty Crocker Note: Doughs made with Gold Medal Wondra may look and feel different. Work dough with hands until it holds together.

ELECTRIC MIXER PASTRY

With Gold Medal Wondra Flour, your electric mixer, and rubber scraper—two minutes to perfect pastry!

One-crust Pastry
1 cup Gold Medal
  Wondra Flour*
½ tsp. salt
⅓ cup plus 1 tbsp.
  shortening or ⅓ cup
  lard
2 tbsp. water

Two-crust Pastry
1¾ cups Gold Medal
  Wondra Flour*
1 tsp. salt
¾ cup shortening or ½
  cup plus 2 tbsp. lard
¼ cup water

In large mixer bowl, stir together flour and salt. Add shortening and mix about 1 min. at low speed, or until shortening is evenly cut in. Scrape bottom and sides of bowl constantly. Gradually add water and continue mixing until all the flour is moistened and dough *begins* to gather into beaters, about 1 min. Scrape bowl constantly. Gather dough together with fingers so it cleans the bowl. (If dough does not cling together, add 1 to 2 tsp. more water.) Press firmly into a ball. On lightly floured cloth-covered board, roll out dough as directed in the meat pie recipe.

*If using Gold Medal Wondra Self-Rising Flour, omit salt.

Betty Crocker Note: When a pastry or biscuit recipe calls for shortening, use the hydrogenated type (such as Crisco, Spry, etc.).

HOMESPUN MEAT PIE

1 small onion, sliced
1 tbsp. shortening
1 lb. beef or veal stew
   meat, cut into 2″ cubes
2 cups boiling water
2 tsp. salt
¼ tsp. pepper
2 medium onions,
   coarsely chopped
1 cup sliced carrots

1 cup fresh or frozen
   green peas
½ cup diced pared
   potatoes
½ cup diced celery
½ cup cold water
¼ cup Gold Medal Flour
   (regular or Wondra)
Stir-n-Roll Biscuits
   (right)

Cook and stir sliced onion in hot shortening until tender. Add meat and brown well on all sides. Add boiling water, salt, and pepper. Cover and simmer over low heat until tender, 2 to 3 hr. During last half hour, add remaining vegetables.

Heat oven to 450°. Remove meat and vegetables from hot broth and place in square pan, 8x8x2″ or 9x9x2″. Skim excess fat from meat broth; measure broth and return to pan. (There should be approximately 2 cups broth.) Shake ½ cup water and the flour together in covered jar. (For a smooth mixture, put water in first, flour on top.) Stir flour and water slowly into hot broth. Heat to boiling, stirring constantly. Boil 1 min. Keep gravy hot while making Stir-n-Roll Biscuits. Pour gravy over meat and vegetables; place biscuits on top. Bake 20 min. *4 or 5 servings.*

STIR-N-ROLL BISCUITS

2 cups Gold Medal Flour
   (regular or Wondra)
3 tsp. baking powder

1 tsp. salt
⅓ cup salad oil
⅔ cup milk

Mix flour, baking powder, and salt in bowl. Pour oil and milk into measuring cup (do not stir together). Pour all at once into dry ingredients. Stir with fork until mixture cleans sides of bowl and forms a ball. To knead: turn dough onto waxed paper; lift paper by one corner and fold dough in half; press down firmly; pull paper back. Repeat 10 times. Pat or roll out dough ½″ thick between 2 sheets of waxed paper. Cut with unfloured 3″ biscuit cutter. *Makes 9 large biscuits.*

BETTY CROCKER NOTE
You may use Gold Medal Self-Rising Flour for any of the biscuit or dumpling recipes in this book. Follow recipe as given except —omit baking powder and salt.

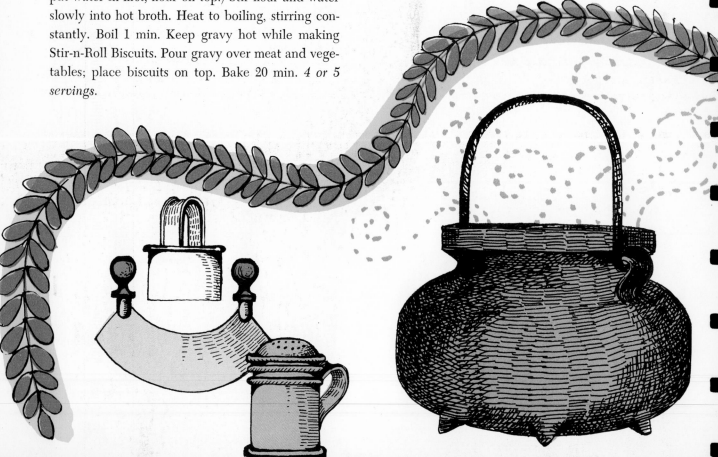

HAM AND POTATO CHIP DUMPLINGS

1 can (10½ oz.) cream
  of chicken soup
½ cup water
1 tbsp. onion flakes
1 can (1 lb.) small green
  Lima beans, drained
1 jar (2 oz.) sliced
  pimiento, drained
  (3 tbsp.)

1 can (12 oz.) chopped
  ham or pork luncheon
  meat, cubed
Potato Chip Dumplings
  (below)
½ cup crushed potato
  chips

Heat oven to 425°. Blend soup, water, and onion flakes in 2-qt. casserole. Stir in Lima beans, pimiento, and ham. Bake uncovered 20 to 25 min. Remove from oven; spoon 7 or 8 dumplings onto hot mixture. Sprinkle with crushed chips. Bake uncovered 20 to 25 min. *6 servings.*

POTATO CHIP DUMPLINGS

1 cup Gold Medal Flour
  (regular or Wondra)
2 tsp. baking powder

¼ tsp. salt
½ cup milk
2 tbsp. salad oil

Mix flour, baking powder, and salt in bowl; add milk and oil all at once and stir just until well blended.

CHEESE CLOUD ON CREAMY CHICKEN

Pretty as can be! See it pictured on p. 87.

1 pkg. (10 oz.) frozen
  green peas,
  cooked and drained
2 cups cubed cooked
  chicken
1 can (10½ oz.) cream
  of chicken soup
1 cup dairy sour cream

½ tsp. salt
⅛ tsp. pepper
1 tbsp. each chopped
  parsley and pimiento
Cheese Cloud (below)
¼ cup shredded natural
  Cheddar cheese
¼ cup milk

Heat oven to 350°. Mix peas and chicken in 2-qt. casserole. Combine soup, sour cream, and seasonings; heat just to boiling. Stir in chopped parsley and pimiento. Add 1½ cups of the soup-cream mixture to peas and chicken; stir to mix. Place casserole in oven to keep warm while preparing Cheese Cloud. Drop spoonfuls of Cheese Cloud over hot mixture. Sprinkle with shredded cheese. Bake 40 to 45 min. Stir milk into remaining soup-cream mixture. Heat and serve as a sauce. Garnish with parsley and pimiento, if desired. *6 to 8 servings.*

CHEESE CLOUD

1 cup Gold Medal Flour*
  (regular or Wondra)
2 tsp. baking powder
1 tsp. salt
2 eggs, beaten

½ cup milk
1 cup shredded natural
  Cheddar cheese
1 tbsp. each chopped
  parsley and pimiento

Stir together flour, baking powder, and salt. Mix eggs, milk, cheese, parsley, and pimiento; stir into dry ingredients just until blended.

*If using Gold Medal Self-Rising Flour, omit baking powder and salt.

BOLOGNA BISCUIT BAKE

¼ cup sliced onion	½ lb. bologna, cubed
2 tbsp. shortening	(2 cups)
2 tbsp. flour	¾ cup diced carrots,
½ tsp. salt	cooked and drained
⅛ tsp. pepper	¾ cup cut green beans,
1 can (1 lb.) tomatoes	cooked and drained
(2 cups)	Bologna Biscuits (below)

Heat oven to 425°. Cook and stir onion in hot shortening until tender. Remove from heat. Blend in flour, salt, and pepper. Cook over low heat, stirring until mixture is bubbly. Remove from heat. Stir in tomatoes. Heat to boiling, stirring constantly. Boil 1 min. Add bologna, carrots, and beans; return to boiling. Pour into square pan, 8x8x2″. Place in oven to keep hot while making Bologna Biscuits. Drop 8 or 9 tablespoonfuls of biscuit dough on hot mixture. Bake 25 to 30 min., or until biscuits are lightly browned. *5 servings.*

BOLOGNA BISCUITS

1 cup Gold Medal Flour	2 tbsp. shortening
(regular or Wondra)	¼ lb. bologna, cut into
1½ tsp. baking powder	¼″ cubes (1 cup)
½ tsp. salt	½ cup milk

Mix flour, baking powder, and salt in bowl; cut in shortening with pastry blender until mixture looks like meal. Stir in bologna cubes, then milk.

Betty Crocker Note: The trick to non-soggy biscuits on meat pies is in the filling! Have the filling good and hot when you top it with biscuits. Our recipes tell you to heat the filling in a skillet or saucepan and, if necessary, to keep hot in the oven while preparing dough.

SIMPLE SIMON SKILLET PIE

¼ cup Gold Medal Flour	8 frankfurters, halved
(regular or Wondra)	lengthwise
2 cans (1 lb. each) seasoned	1 can of our refrigerated
stewed tomatoes	biscuits
½ cup sliced pitted ripe	1 cup shredded Cheddar
olives	cheese

Stir flour into tomatoes and olives in skillet. Heat to boiling, stirring constantly. Add frankfurters. Cut biscuits into quarters and place on top of tomato mixture. Sprinkle with cheese. Cover and simmer gently 30 min. *4 to 6 servings.*

Betty Crocker Note: To cut biscuits, snip them with kitchen scissors.

TUNA WITH CALICO CORN MUFFINS

Tuna and broccoli bake under corn muffins flecked with green pepper and pimiento. So bright and gay and delicious, you'll want to make this a company special! Pictured opposite.

2 pkg. (10 oz. each)	¼ tsp. dry mustard
frozen broccoli spears	¼ cup chopped green
2 cans (6½ oz. each)	pepper
tuna, drained	¼ cup chopped pimiento
1 pkg. of our corn	2 cans (10½ oz. each)
muffin mix	cream of mushroom
¾ tsp. salt	soup
½ tsp. sage	

Heat oven to 400°. Cook broccoli in 1 cup boiling *unsalted* water 5 min.; drain well. Arrange broccoli in oblong baking dish, 13x9½x2″; cover with tuna. Prepare muffin mix as directed on package except— stir in the salt, sage, mustard, green pepper, and pimiento with the dry mix. Quickly heat soup to boiling; pour over tuna. Drop spoonfuls of muffin batter onto hot soup. Bake 30 to 35 min., or until top is golden. Garnish with green pepper rings and ripe olives, if desired. *8 to 10 servings.*

Pictured from top to bottom: Tuna wtih Calico Corn Muffins, Cheese Cloud on Creamy Chicken, Creamy Beef with Chive Biscuits

CREAMY BEEF WITH CHIVE BISCUITS

Meat and vegetables richly flavored with sour cream. See it pictured on p. 87.

½ cup Bisquick	3 large carrots, sliced
½ tsp. salt	1 small clove garlic,
⅛ tsp. pepper	minced
⅛ tsp. paprika	⅔ cup dairy sour cream
1½ lb. beef stew meat,	¼ tsp. Worcestershire
cut into 2″ cubes	sauce
1 to 2 tbsp. shortening	Salt and pepper
½ cup canned tomatoes	Sour Cream Chive
2 small onions, chopped	Biscuits (below)

Mix Bisquick, ½ tsp. salt, ⅛ tsp. pepper, and the paprika; coat meat with this mixture. In large skillet or Dutch oven, brown meat well on all sides in hot shortening. Add vegetables, garlic, and enough water to cover meat and vegetables. Cover tightly; cook over low heat until meat is tender, about 2 hr. (Add more water, if necessary.)

Heat oven to 425°. Remove skillet from heat; stir in sour cream and Worcestershire sauce. Season to taste with salt and pepper. Pour into 2-qt. casserole; place in oven to keep hot while making biscuits. Place biscuits on hot mixture. Bake 15 to 20 min., or until biscuits are a delicate golden brown. *4 to 6 servings.*

SOUR CREAM CHIVE BISCUITS

Stir 2 cups Bisquick, ⅔ cup dairy sour cream, ⅓ cup water, and 1 tbsp. chopped chives to a soft dough. Beat vigorously 20 strokes until stiff but sticky. Roll dough on floured cloth-covered board. Knead 8 to 10 times. Roll out ½″ thick. Cut with floured 2″ cutter.

BEEF STEW WITH POTATO CRUST

1½ cups Gold Medal Flour*	⅓ cup shortening
(regular or Wondra)	¼ cup milk or water
2 tsp. baking powder	2 cans (1½ lb. each)
½ tsp. salt	beef stew or 5 cups
¾ cup cold mashed potatoes	beef stew

Heat oven to 450°. Mix flour, baking powder, and salt. Cut in potatoes and shortening with pastry blender until particles are the size of peas. Stir in milk. On lightly floured cloth-covered board, roll out dough to fit top of 2-qt. casserole. (Dough will be quite thick, about ½″.) Cut slits for steam to escape. Quickly heat stew to simmering; pour into casserole. Place round of potato dough on top. Bake 20 to 25 min. *6 to 8 servings.*

*If using Gold Medal Self-Rising Flour, omit baking powder and salt.

Betty Crocker Note: You're sure to have a topping that fits when you invert the casserole on dough and trim around it.

Beans—*Naturally nourishing and tasty—with cheese, apples, tomatoes, or pork.*

APPLE ORCHARD BEAN BAKE

1 lb. bulk pork sausage
1 can (1 lb. 4 oz.) pork and beans in molasses sauce
½ can (10½ oz.) tomato soup
¼ tsp. pepper
1 large unpared apple, cored and very thinly sliced
¼ cup brown sugar (packed)

Heat oven to 450°. Brown sausage in skillet. Drain off excess fat. Stir in beans, soup, and pepper; pour into 1½-qt. casserole. Arrange apple slices over top; sprinkle with brown sugar. Bake uncovered 25 min. Remove from oven; let stand 5 to 10 min. until beans absorb juices. *6 servings.*

SNAPPY LIMA CASSEROLE

1½ cups dried Lima beans (¾ lb.)
1 lb. pork sausage links
¾ cup chopped onion
¼ cup finely chopped green pepper
1 can (10½ oz.) tomato soup
2 tbsp. molasses
1 tbsp. brown sugar
1½ tsp. salt
½ tsp. dry mustard
½ cup shredded sharp Cheddar cheese

In large kettle, cover beans with water; heat to boiling. Simmer 2 min. Remove from heat; cover and let stand 1 hr. Return to heat. Simmer 45 to 60 min., or until beans are tender. (Add more water to cover beans, if necessary.) Drain.

Heat oven to 350°. Lightly brown sausages in skillet. Remove all but 1 to 2 tbsp. fat from skillet. Cook and stir onion and green pepper in hot fat until onion is tender. Stir in drained Lima beans, soup, molasses, brown sugar, salt, and mustard. Pour into 1½-qt. casserole. Arrange browned sausages spoke-fashion on top; sprinkle with cheese. Cover; bake 20 to 25 min., or until hot and bubbly. *6 servings.*

LENTIL-SAUSAGE CASSEROLE

1½ cups dry lentils
2 cups water
2 tbsp. minced parsley or 1 tbsp. parsley flakes
1 bay leaf
½ tsp. salt
1 lb. bulk pork sausage
½ cup chopped onion
1 stalk celery (with leaves), chopped
1 clove garlic, minced
2 tbsp. flour
1 can (1 lb. 4 oz.) tomatoes
½ cup grated Parmesan cheese

Cover lentils with water. Add parsley, bay leaf, and salt. Cover and simmer 30 to 45 min., or until lentils are tender. (Add more water, if necessary. Water should be absorbed at the end of the cooking period.)

Heat oven to 350°. Brown sausage in large skillet. Pour all but 3 to 4 tbsp. fat from skillet. Add onion, celery, and garlic; cook and stir until onion is tender. Remove from heat. Blend in flour. Cook over low heat, stirring until mixture is bubbly. Remove from heat. Stir in tomatoes. Heat to boiling, stirring constantly. Simmer 1 min. Combine lentil and sausage mixtures in 2-qt. casserole. Sprinkle with Parmesan cheese. Cover and bake 15 min.; uncover and bake 15 min. longer. Remove from oven; let stand 5 to 10 min. *6 servings.*

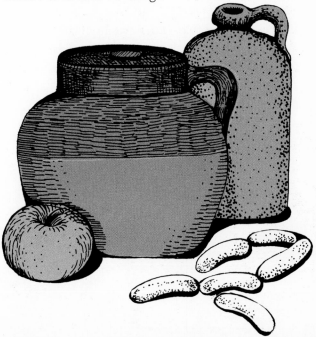

Pot Roast—*Especially delicious with dill, Italian-style, or cooked in aluminum foil.*

DILLY OF A POT ROAST

The delightful difference here is a pot roast with zucchini to spark up carrots and potatoes—all seasoned with dill and served with a luscious sour cream gravy.

2 tbsp. flour	5 small potatoes, pared
1 tsp. salt	5 carrots, quartered
¼ tsp. pepper	½ tsp. salt
2½-lb. beef pot roast	1 lb. zucchini squash, quartered
1 tbsp. shortening	
¼ cup water	½ tsp. salt
1 tbsp. vinegar	Sour Cream Gravy (below)
1 tsp. dill weed	

Mix flour, 1 tsp. salt, and the pepper; rub meat with flour mixture. Brown well in hot shortening in large heavy skillet or Dutch oven. Add water and vinegar. Sprinkle ½ tsp. dill weed over meat; turn meat and sprinkle with remaining ½ tsp. dill weed. Cover; simmer 1½ to 2 hr. Add potatoes and carrots; sprinkle with ½ tsp. salt. Cover and simmer 40 min. Add zucchini; sprinkle with ½ tsp. salt. Cover and simmer 20 min., or until vegetables are tender. Remove meat and vegetables to a platter and keep warm while making Sour Cream Gravy. *4 to 6 servings.*

SOUR CREAM GRAVY
Measure meat broth. (If necessary, add enough water to make 1 cup liquid.) Mix 1 cup dairy sour cream, 1 tbsp. flour, and 1 tsp. dill weed in skillet; gradually stir in meat broth. Heat *just* to boiling, stirring constantly.

SUNDAY BEST POT ROAST

½ cup Gold Medal Flour (regular or Wondra)	8 to 10 medium carrots
1 tsp. salt	8 to 10 stalks celery, cut up
½ tsp. paprika	8 to 10 small pared potatoes or 4 large potatoes, pared and quartered
¼ tsp. pepper	
4- to 5-lb. beef pot roast	
2 tbsp. shortening	
1 cup water	1 tsp. salt
8 to 10 small onions	Pot Roast Gravy (below)

Mix flour, 1 tsp. salt, paprika, and the pepper; rub meat with flour mixture. Brown well in hot shortening in large heavy Dutch oven or skillet. Add water. Cover tightly and simmer 3½ to 4 hr., or until meat is tender. About 45 min. before roast is done, add vegetables; sprinkle with 1 tsp. salt. Continue simmering until meat and vegetables are tender. Remove meat and vegetables to hot platter; keep warm while making Pot Roast Gravy. *8 to 10 servings.*

POT ROAST GRAVY
Skim excess fat from meat broth. Measure broth and return to pan. For each cup of broth, mix ¼ cup cold water with 2 tablespoons flour. Gradually stir into hot broth. Heat to boiling, stirring constantly. Boil 1 min. Season; serve in a separate bowl.

POT ROAST ITALIANO

Team up with crisp Zucchini Toss (p.149).

2- to 3-lb. beef pot roast	**1 pkg. of our noodles**
Salt and pepper	**Italiano**
1 tbsp. shortening	**2 tbsp. butter or margarine**
¾ cup hot water	**¼ cup hot water**

Season meat with salt and pepper; brown well in hot shortening. Blend ¾ cup water into tomato sauce mix from package of noodles Italiano; pour over meat. Cover; simmer 2 hr., or until tender. Spoon sauce over meat occasionally while cooking. (If sauce thickens, add water.) Cook and drain noodles as directed on package. Blend in butter, packet of cheese mix, and ¼ cup water. Arrange meat and noodles on serving platter. Serve with sauce. *4 servings.*

SHORT RIBS JARDINIERE

Richly flavored meat and vegetables accented with the zip of horseradish. A man's dinner!

⅓ cup Gold Medal Flour	**½ cup hot water**
(regular or Wondra)	**2 tsp. horseradish**
2 tsp. salt	**6 small carrots**
½ tsp. pepper	**4 medium onions**
2 lb. lean short ribs, cut	**2 stalks celery, cut into**
into individual servings	**2″ lengths**
2 tbsp. shortening	**Salt and pepper**

Mix flour, 2 tsp. salt, and ½ tsp. pepper; coat meat with flour mixture. In large heavy skillet or Dutch oven, brown meat well in hot shortening. Drain off excess fat. Add the water and horseradish. Cover tightly and simmer slowly about 2 hr., or until meat is tender. Add more water, if necessary. Add vegetables and season lightly with salt and pepper. Cover; cook 30 to 40 min. longer, or until vegetables are tender. *4 servings.*

STEAK SUPPER IN A FOIL PACKAGE

1½ lb. chuck steak, 1″	**3 medium carrots,**
thick	**quartered**
1 can (10½ oz.) cream of	**2 stalks celery, cut into**
mushroom or cream of	**2″ lengths**
celery soup	**2 to 3 medium potatoes,**
1 envelope (1½ oz.)	**pared and quartered**
dehydrated onion	**2 tbsp. water**
soup mix	

Heat oven to 450°. Tear off 2 feet of heavy-duty aluminum foil, 18″ wide; lay in baking pan. Place meat in center. Mix mushroom soup and onion soup mix; spread over meat. Top with vegetables. Sprinkle vegetables with water. Fold foil over and seal securely to hold in juices. Bake 1½ hr., or until meat is tender. *4 servings.*

NEW ENGLAND "BOILED" DINNER

When it comes to "just plain good eating," nothing is better than flavorful corned beef and cabbage!

3- to 4-lb. corned brisket	**2 turnips, cubed**
of beef	**(optional)**
8 small onions	**1 head green cabbage,**
8 whole carrots	**cut into 8 wedges**
4 potatoes, pared and	**Freshly ground pepper**
halved	

Place beef in heavy kettle; cover with hot water. Cover tightly; simmer 3 to 3½ hr., or until tender. Skim off excess fat; add onions, carrots, potatoes, and turnips. Cover and simmer 20 min. Add cabbage and simmer 10 to 15 min. longer, or until vegetables are tender. Arrange meat and vegetables on a platter and sprinkle with pepper. *8 servings.*

Pork Chops—*Barbecued, "tomatoed," or glazed with fruit juice.*

INDIAN CHOPS

Thick pork chops with creamy wild rice—an easy-to-prepare gourmet dish that appeals to hearty masculine appetites.

4 pork chops, 1½"
   thick
1 tsp. dry mustard
1 tsp. ground cloves
1 can (10½ oz.) cream
   of mushroom soup
½ cup water
¼ cup red Burgundy

1 can (6 oz.) mushroom
   crowns, drained
   (reserve liquid)
3 cups hot cooked
   wild rice
4 large slices white onion
4 large slices tomato

Trim excess fat from chops. Rub chops with mixture of mustard and cloves. Grease hot electric skillet with fat from one chop. Brown chops slowly on both sides. Drain off any excess fat. Mix soup, water, Burgundy, and mushroom liquid in a bowl; stir in rice and mix well. Place an onion slice on each chop. Pour rice mixture over the chops and top with mushrooms. Cover and simmer 1½ hr., or until chops are done—no pink in center. Stir mixture around the edges occasionally. During the last 30 min. of cooking, place a slice of tomato on top of each onion slice. *4 servings.*

TO-PO PORK CHOPS

Hearty meat and potato skillet meal, delightfully flavored with tomatoes and basil. Serve with oven-toasted garlic bread.

6 pork chops, ¾" thick
½ tsp. salt
¼ tsp. pepper
1 can (1 lb.) tomatoes
¼ cup water
1 tsp. salt

¾ tsp. crushed basil
⅛ tsp. pepper
4 medium potatoes, pared
   and cut into ⅛" slices
1 medium onion, sliced

Trim excess fat from chops; lightly grease heavy skillet with fat from one chop. Brown chops slowly on both sides; season each side with ¼ tsp. salt and ⅛ tsp. pepper. Remove chops; drain fat from skillet. Add tomatoes to skillet; break up with fork. Mix in water, 1 tsp. salt, the basil, and ⅛ tsp. pepper. Layer potatoes in tomato mixture. Arrange onion over potatoes. Top with chops. Cover tightly; simmer 45 min., or until potatoes are tender and chops are done—no pink in center. *6 servings.*

PORK CHOP SCALLOP

4 pork chops, ¾" thick
Flour
Salt and pepper

1 pkg. of our scalloped
   potatoes
2 cups water
½ cup milk

Trim excess fat from chops; dip in flour. Lightly grease heavy 10" skillet with fat from one chop. Brown chops slowly on both sides; season with salt and pepper. Remove chops. Drain off excess fat. Empty potatoes and seasoned sauce mix into skillet. Stir in water and milk. Place pork chops on top. Heat to boiling. Cover and simmer 30 to 35 min., or until chops are done—no pink in center. Garnish with parsley, if desired. *4 servings.*

PORK POT ORANGÉ

Orange-glazed pork chops with sweet potatoes and onions; pictured below.

6 pork chops, 1″ thick	**2 tbsp. lemon juice**
1½ tsp. salt	**½ tsp. salt**
¼ tsp. pepper	**2 lb. sweet potatoes or**
1 onion, cut into 6 slices	**yams, pared and cut**
⅓ cup brown sugar	**into ½″ slices**
(packed)	**6 thin orange slices**
½ cup water	**1 tbsp. cornstarch**
1 tsp. grated orange peel	**¼ cup cold water**
⅓ cup orange juice	

Trim excess fat from chops; lightly grease heavy skillet with fat from one chop. Brown chops slowly on one side; turn and sprinkle with ¾ tsp. salt and ⅛ tsp. pepper. Brown other side of chops; turn and sprinkle the meat with ¾ tsp. salt and ⅛ tsp. pepper. Drain off any excess fat. Top each chop with an onion slice. Mix brown sugar, ½ cup water, the orange peel, orange juice, lemon juice, and ½ tsp. salt. Pour over chops. Cover and simmer 30 min. Lift chops and arrange sweet potato slices in sauce. Replace chops; top each onion slice with an orange slice. Cover; simmer 45 min., or until potatoes are tender and chops are done—no pink in center. Remove chops and sweet potatoes to a heated platter; keep warm. Blend cornstarch and ¼ cup water; stir into sauce in skillet. Cook, stirring constantly, until mixture thickens and boils. Boil and stir 1 min. Pour over chops and sweet potatoes on platter. *6 servings.*

BARBECUE BANQUET IN A SKILLET

Tastes like a barbecue—indoors or out—all year 'round. Your only additions—a big tossed salad, Corn Muffins (p. 152), wedges of luscious devils food cake.

6 pork chops, ¾″ thick	**1 tsp. salt**
1 cup uncooked	**6 large onion slices**
regular rice	**6 lemon slices**
3 cups tomato juice	**6 tbsp. brown sugar**
½ tsp. Tabasco	**6 tbsp. catsup**

Trim excess fat from chops; lightly grease heavy skillet with fat from one chop. Brown chops slowly on both sides. Remove chops and pour off all the excess fat. Stir in rice, tomato juice, and Tabasco; mix well. Arrange the chops on top and sprinkle with salt. Place a slice of onion, a slice of lemon, a tablespoonful of brown sugar, and a tablespoonful of catsup on each chop. Cover tightly and simmer slowly over low heat 40 min., or until rice is cooked and chops are done—no pink in center. *6 servings.*

Stuffed Vegetables—*Flavorful meat-and-vegetable medleys in colorful shells.*

STUFFED PEPPERS FESTIVO

1 pkg. of our macaroni and Cheddar
1 cup cubed cooked ham
4 large or 6 medium green peppers

Heat oven to 350°. Prepare our macaroni and Cheddar as directed on package for range top method. Stir in ham. Cut thin slice from stem end of each pepper; remove all seeds and membranes. Wash outside and inside. Cook in boiling salted water 5 min.; drain well. Stuff peppers with macaroni mixture. Stand upright in baking dish. Cover; bake 30 min. Garnish with green onion tops and parsley, if desired. *4 to 6 servings.*

STUFFED EGGPLANT PARMIGIANA

2 small eggplants or 1 medium eggplant
1 lb. bulk pork sausage or Italian sausage*
1 can (1 lb.) tomatoes
1 can (6 oz.) tomato paste
2 tbsp. minced parsley
1 tbsp. minced onion
1 clove garlic, minced
½ tsp. salt
½ tsp. crushed oregano
1 cup shredded mozzarella cheese (4 oz.)
½ cup grated or shredded Parmesan cheese

Heat oven to 350°. Cut eggplants in half. Scoop out pulp; dice. Brown sausage in skillet; drain on paper towels. Drain excess fat from skillet. Combine sausage, tomatoes, tomato paste, parsley, and seasonings in skillet. Cover and simmer 15 min. Add diced eggplant pulp; cover and simmer 15 min. longer. Place eggplant shells in oblong baking dish. 13x9½x2″. Fill shells half full with sauce. Sprinkle with mozzarella cheese. Heap remaining sauce in shells and sprinkle with Parmesan cheese. Bake uncovered 30 min. Garnish with hot peppers, if desired. *4 servings.*

*Remove casing from Italian sausage before browning.

FRUITED BAKED SQUASH

Ham and squash accented with the tang of fruit.

2 acorn squash
2 cups cubed cooked ham
1 small orange, finely chopped (pulp and peel)
1 cup chopped unpared apple
¼ cup brown sugar (packed)
¼ cup soft butter or margarine
Salt

Heat oven to 400°. Cut squash in half crosswise; scoop out seeds. Place cut side down in baking pan. Pour in water to ¼″ depth. Bake 30 min. Mix ham, orange, apple, brown sugar, and butter. Turn squash cut side up; sprinkle lightly with salt. Fill squash halves with ham mixture. Bake 30 min., or until squash is tender. Garnish with twist of orange, if desired. *4 servings.*

Macaroni and Cheese—*Old-fashioned favorite glorified with new flavors.*

MACARONI WITH CHEESE AND BEEF

Creamy macaroni and cheese with butter-browned dried beef.

4 oz. dried beef, shredded	**7 or 8 oz. elbow macaroni, cooked and drained**
2 tbsp. butter or margarine	**2 eggs, well beaten**
2 cups shredded sharp Cheddar cheese (8 oz.)	**2½ cups milk**
½ to 1 tsp. celery seed	**¼ cup buttered bread crumbs**

Heat oven to 350°. Cook and stir dried beef in butter until edges curl. Mix cheese and celery seed with macaroni. Layer macaroni and beef in buttered 2-qt. casserole. Mix eggs and milk. Pour over macaroni. Bake 30 min. Top with crumbs and bake 15 min. longer. *4 to 6 servings.*

POLKA-DOTTED MACARONI AND CHEESE

Sauced in no time with a can of cheese soup!

7 oz. macaroni, cooked and drained	**1 can (11 oz.) Cheddar cheese soup**
½ cup milk	**2 frankfurters, cut into penny-thin slices**
1 tsp. Worcestershire sauce	

Heat oven to 375°. Spread macaroni in oblong baking dish, 10x6x1½″. Blend milk and Worcestershire sauce with soup. Pour over macaroni, stirring to mix. Arrange frankfurter slices on top of macaroni and cheese. Bake 25 min., or until mixture is hot and bubbly. *4 to 6 servings.*

MACARONI TUNA PIE

1 stick of our pie crust mix	**1 can (6½ oz.) tuna, drained**
1 tsp. celery seed	**1 tomato, cut into thin slices**
1 pkg. of our macaroni and Cheddar	

Prepare 9″ baked pie shell as directed on inside wrapper except—add celery seed to crumbled mix.

Heat oven to 375°. Prepare macaroni and Cheddar as directed on package for range-top method except—remove from heat as soon as sauce comes to boiling (do not boil the 2 min.); stir in tuna. Pour into baked pie shell. Arrange tomato slices in circle around top edge of pie. Bake 10 min. Garnish with parsley, if desired. *4 to 6 servings.*

Square-meal Suppers—*"Stick-to-the-ribs" satisfaction for man-sized appetites.*

STUFFED SPARERIBS WITH YAMMY APPLES

Meat and stuffing, potatoes and fruit—a dinner deliciously complete.

4 lb. spareribs	1 cup chopped celery
Salt and pepper	½ cup chopped onion
1½ cups coarsely crumbled packaged herb seasoned stuffing	¼ cup water
	Yammy Apples (below)

Heat oven to 350°. Cut ribs into 8 equal sections; season on both sides with salt and pepper. Combine stuffing, celery, onion, and water. Place 4 of the rib sections meat side down on a rack in a large roaster. Mound ¼ of the stuffing on each section; do not pack. Place remaining sections meat side up over stuffing. Cover pan; bake 1½ hr. Place Yammy Apples on rack next to the ribs; bake uncovered 1 hr. longer, until apples are tender. *4 servings.*

YAMMY APPLES

4 medium baking apples	1 tbsp. butter or margarine, melted
1 can (8 oz.) sweet potatoes, drained and mashed	½ tsp. cinnamon
	¼ tsp. salt
3 tbsp. brown sugar	3 tbsp. slivered almonds
3 tbsp. maple syrup	

Wash and core apples; remove enough pulp to make the opening about 2" wide. Chop the pulp and mix with remaining ingredients except 1 tbsp. almonds. Wrap a 7" square of aluminum foil around bottom and sides of each apple. Fill cavities with sweet potato mixture; stud with remaining almonds.

SPICY STUFFED VEAL

Thin veal steaks, each wrapped around a flavorful sausage and simmered in stewed tomatoes.

4 pork sausage links	½ cup uncooked regular rice
¾ lb. thin veal steak	
2 tbsp. flour	1 can (1 lb.) stewed tomatoes
1 tsp. salt	
1 medium onion, sliced	2 tsp. sugar
	1 tsp. salt

Lightly brown sausages in large heavy skillet. Remove and drain on paper towels. Cut veal into 4 pieces; wrap each piece around a sausage; fasten with wooden pick. Roll in mixture of flour and 1 tsp. salt. Brown veal rolls on all sides in hot sausage fat in skillet. Remove veal rolls; drain on paper towels. Drain fat from skillet. Add the remaining ingredients; mix well. Add veal rolls. Cover; simmer, stirring occasionally, about 40 min., or until veal rolls and rice are tender and liquid has been absorbed. Remove wooden picks from meat before serving. *4 servings.*

COUNTRY-STYLE LIVER

4 slices bacon	1 cup sliced carrots
3 tbsp. flour	1 cup sliced celery
¼ tsp. crushed marjoram	2 cups sliced onion
¼ tsp. poultry seasoning	2 medium potatoes, pared and quartered
¼ tsp. salt	
¼ tsp. pepper	1 cup tomato juice
1 lb. sliced beef liver	½ tsp. salt

Fry bacon until crisp; remove and drain on paper towels. Mix flour and next 4 seasonings; coat liver with flour mixture. Brown liver in bacon drippings; drain off excess fat. Arrange the vegetables over browned liver. Pour tomato juice over and sprinkle with ½ tsp. salt. Cover and simmer 30 to 40 min., or until vegetables are tender. Crumble bacon and sprinkle over top. *4 servings.*

SOUTHERN LAMB SHANK DINNER

Pictured below with Celery Coleslaw (p. 150).

¼ cup Gold Medal Flour (regular or Wondra)	¼ cup water
1 tsp. salt	4 medium potatoes, pared and sliced ½" thick
¼ tsp. pepper	
4 lamb shanks	Salt
2 tbsp. shortening	1 can (1 lb.) whole green beans, drained
Barbecue Sauce (below)	

Heat oven to 350°. Mix flour, 1 tsp. salt, and the pepper; rub shanks with flour mixture. Brown meat well in hot shortening in Dutch oven. Drain off excess fat. Brush meat with Barbecue Sauce. Add water to pan. Cover and bake 1 hr. Brush meat with sauce again; add potatoes and season with salt. Cover; bake 1 hr. longer. Brush remaining sauce over meat; add beans and bake uncovered 30 min. *4 servings.*

BARBECUE SAUCE

½ cup catsup	Dash Tabasco
2 tbsp. brown sugar	1 clove garlic, minced
2 tbsp. Worcestershire sauce	¼ tsp. dry mustard
1 tbsp. vinegar	¼ tsp. salt

Combine ingredients in saucepan; cook and stir over low heat 5 min.

PINEAPPLE LAMB CHOPS

The pineapple syrup caramelizes on potatoes and mushrooms, adding wonderful flavor and color. A good idea for company dinners, too.

4 shoulder lamb chops, ½ to ¾" thick	1 can (8½ oz.) sliced pineapple, drained (reserve syrup)
Salt and pepper	
4 small to medium potatoes, pared and sliced ½" thick	Salt and pepper
	½ to 1 tsp. crushed basil
1 can (4 oz.) button mushrooms, drained	1 to 2 tbsp. butter or margarine

Trim fat from chops; lightly grease heavy skillet with fat from one chop. Brown meat on both sides; season with salt and pepper. Remove chops and drain off fat. Layer potatoes and mushrooms in skillet; cover with browned chops. Top each chop with a pineapple ring. Add enough water to reserved pineapple syrup to make ½ cup; pour over chops. Season with salt, pepper, and basil; dot with butter. Cover and cook over low heat about 40 min., or until chops are well done and potatoes are tender. (Add more water, if necessary, *or* if there is excessive liquid, remove cover and cook until liquid evaporates.) *4 servings.*

BEEF RING WITH MASHED POTATOES

Most of the meal is on the platter! To complete, serve a plate of chilled tomato slices sprinkled with dill and a basket of thick-crusted bread.

1 lb. ground beef	1 pkg. of our
¼ cup dry bread crumbs	mashed Potato Buds
½ cup milk	Cheddar cheese strips
1 tsp. salt	1 pkg. (10 oz.) frozen
3 tbsp. catsup	green beans or peas,
2 tbsp. finely chopped	cooked and drained
onion	Butter
1½ tsp. Worcestershire	
sauce	

Heat oven to 350°. Mix ground beef, bread crumbs, milk, and seasonings. Form meat mixture into a ring in 9″ pie pan, leaving center large enough for the mashed potatoes. Bake 30 min. Prepare potatoes as directed on package for 4 servings. Remove meat from oven. (If drippings have accumulated in center, use a baster to remove before adding potatoes. Drippings may be used for gravy, if desired.) Fill center of ring with potatoes. Place strips of cheese over potatoes. Bake 10 min. longer, or until cheese melts. Butter green vegetables and arrange around meat ring. *4 servings.*

CHICKEN OF SIX SEASONINGS

Count them! Six seasonings add up to a blend of exceptional flavor.

¼ cup Gold Medal Flour	⅓ cup chopped onion
(regular or Wondra)	1 can (4 oz.) mushroom
1 tsp. salt	stems and pieces,
½ tsp. parsley flakes	drained (reserve liquid)
¼ tsp. pepper	1 can (1 lb.) tomatoes
¼ tsp. crushed thyme	1 tbsp. brown sugar
¼ tsp. crushed rosemary	1 tbsp. lemon juice
¼ tsp. crushed oregano	1 tsp. salt
2½- to 3-lb. broiler-fryer	¾ cup uncooked regular
chicken, cut up	rice
¼ cup shortening	

Mix flour and next 6 seasonings in a paper bag. Place a few chicken pieces in the bag and shake well; repeat until all chicken is coated. (Reserve seasoned flour for thickening.) Starting with meaty pieces, brown chicken in hot shortening 15 to 20 min. Remove browned chicken and drain on paper towels. Add onion and mushrooms to skillet; cook and stir until onion is tender. Remove from heat. Stir in reserved seasoned flour; add tomatoes, mushroom liquid, brown sugar, lemon juice, 1 tsp. salt, and rice. Heat to boiling, stirring constantly. Add chicken; cover and simmer 40 min., or until rice and chicken are tender. *6 servings.*

FRANKLY PEPPERED POTATO BAKE

1 cup chopped onion	2 tsp. caraway seed,
3 tbsp. butter or	if desired
margarine	2 tsp. paprika
¼ tsp. garlic powder	1 tsp. salt
2 small green peppers, cut	1 can (10½ oz.) tomato
into 1″ pieces (2 cups)	soup
3 cups diced pared	1 lb. frankfurters, cut
potatoes	into ½″ slices

Heat oven to 350°. Cook and stir onion in butter until tender. Add remaining ingredients; mix well. Pour into oblong baking dish, 11½x7½x1½″. Cover with aluminum foil. Bake 1 hr. 15 min. *6 servings.*

EASY SCALLOPED POTATOES AND HAM

3 tbsp. flour	¼ cup minced onion
½ tsp. salt	½ lb. ham, sliced
⅛ tsp. pepper	2½ cups milk, scalded
4 cups thinly sliced pared	1 tbsp. butter
potatoes	

Heat oven to 350°. Mix flour, salt, and pepper. Place ⅓ of the potatoes in 2-qt. greased casserole. Sprinkle with half the seasoned flour and onion; add half the ham. Repeat; then arrange third layer of potatoes on top. Pour hot milk over all. Dot with butter. Cover and bake 30 min. Uncover and bake 60 to 70 min. longer, or until potatoes are tender. *6 servings.*

POTATO SAUERKRAUT DINNER

1 pkg. of our scalloped	½ tsp. caraway seed
potatoes	1 pkg. (12 oz.) smoked
2¾ cups water	pork sausage links
1 can (1 lb.) sauerkraut	

Empty potatoes and sauce mix into medium skillet. Stir in water; heat to boiling. Cover and simmer 30 min., or until potatoes are tender. Stir in sauerkraut; sprinkle with caraway seed. Arrange sausages on top. Cover and cook over medium heat 10 min. longer. *4 servings.*

STEAK AND POTATO SKILLET

3 tbsp. flour	1 beef bouillon cube
1 tsp. salt	¼ cup catsup
½ tsp. crushed marjoram	1 tbsp. Worcestershire
¼ tsp. pepper	sauce
1½ lb. round steak, cut	2 tsp. bell pepper flakes
into serving pieces	1 pkg. (10 oz.) frozen
1 tbsp. shortening	Italian green beans,
1 cup chopped onion	broken apart
1 can (1 lb.) whole	
potatoes, drained	
(reserve liquid)	

Mix flour, salt, marjoram, and pepper; pound into both sides of steak. Brown meat well on both sides in hot shortening. Add onion; cook and stir until tender. Remove from heat. Add enough water to reserved potato liquid to make 1 cup; mix with bouillon cube, catsup, Worcestershire sauce, and pepper flakes. Pour over meat; heat, stirring until bouillon cube is dissolved. Cover and simmer 1¼ hr., or until meat is tender. Add potatoes and beans. Heat to boiling; cover and simmer 10 min. longer, stirring occasionally, until potatoes are heated through and beans are cooked. *4 servings.*

PEPPER STEAK

Pictured below.

1½ lb. sirloin steak, ½″ thick	2 green peppers, cut into 1″ pieces
½ tsp. salt	2 tbsp. cornstarch
1 cup diced onion	¼ cup cold water
1 cup beef bouillon*	2 tomatoes, peeled and cut into eighths
3 tbsp. soy sauce	
1 clove garlic, minced	3 to 4 cups hot cooked rice

Trim any fat and bone from meat. Cut meat into 4 to 6 serving-size pieces. Grease skillet lightly with fat from meat. Brown meat thoroughly on one side; turn. Sprinkle with ¼ tsp. salt. Brown other side of meat; turn. Sprinkle with remaining ¼ tsp. salt. Push meat to side of skillet. Add onion; cook and stir until tender. Add bouillon, soy sauce, and garlic; cover and simmer 10 min., or until meat is tender. Add green pepper; cover and simmer 5 min. Blend cornstarch with water; gradually stir into mixture in skillet. Cook, stirring constantly, until mixture thickens and boils. Boil and stir 1 min. Add tomatoes; heat through. Serve immediately with hot rice. *4 to 6 servings.*

*Beef bouillon may be made by dissolving 1 beef bouillon cube in 1 cup boiling water, or use canned beef broth.

STEAK ROLL-UPS

Bread Stuffing (below)	½ tsp. salt
4 medium cube steaks	8 small white onions, peeled
3 tbsp. shortening	
1 can (15 oz.) tomato sauce	1 can (1 lb.) French-style green beans, drained
1 tbsp. sugar	

Spread Bread Stuffing over cube steaks; roll and fasten with wooden picks. Brown rolls on all sides in hot shortening. Stir in tomato sauce, sugar, salt, and onions. Cover and simmer 30 to 40 min., or until meat is tender. Add green beans; cover and simmer 10 min. Remove wooden picks from meat rolls just before serving. *4 servings.*

BREAD STUFFING

1 tbsp. minced onion	¼ tsp. each poultry seasoning, crushed thyme, and rosemary
2 tbsp. butter or margarine	
1 cup soft bread cubes	
2 tbsp. chopped celery	Dash pepper
¼ tsp. salt	

Cook and stir onion in butter until tender. Add bread cubes. Heat, stirring to prevent excessive browning. Mix in remaining ingredients. For dry stuffing, add little or no liquid. For moist stuffing, mix in lightly with fork just enough hot water or beef broth to moisten bread cubes.

Simmered and Savory

Here are time-honored meals in a dish at their basic best. Soups, stews, and chowders—these golden medleys of long-simmered goodness have become the great classic dishes of all times and countries.

When you want a meal to remember on a blustery winter day or one to give a satisfying lift to a day of housecleaning, these are the dishes to serve. Put on the soup kettle, the iron skillet, or Dutch oven and take your cue from the Irish farmwife whose steaming stew waits always at a simmer for her hungry menfolk.

These dishes, neither elegant nor dainty, promise the rich nourishment of tender meat or fish and vegetables in flavorful broths from which few valuable vitamins or minerals are lost.

From the International Soup Tureen—
Here are soups and stews adapted from the favorites of other lands—especially for you!

TO SERVE FRENCH STYLE
Top the hot flavorful broth with croutons and serve before your meal-in-one platter of meat and vegetables. (In some French households, the meat course is served for lunch, the broth later in the day as a supper specialty.)

For a sharp accent, pass Dijon-style mustard, horseradish, and tiny sour gherkin pickles with the meat course.

POT-AU-FEU

This is the French version of the pot roast. Traditionally, it is the pot that simmers on the back of the stove.

2 lb. "boiling" beef (brisket, rump, or chuck roast)	1 bay leaf
	1 clove garlic, crushed
	1 sprig parsley
½ lb. marrow bone, cracked	1 turnip, quartered
2½ qt. cold water	4 carrots, halved
1 carrot, diced	4 leeks, halved (trim to within 1″ above white end)
1 stalk celery, diced	
¼ cup chopped onion	
2 tsp. salt	2 stalks celery, halved
5 peppercorns	1 whole onion (insert 3 whole cloves)
1 tsp. crushed thyme	

Place meat, bone, and water in large kettle; add diced carrot and celery, chopped onion, and next 6 seasonings. Heat to boiling; simmer gently uncovered 3 hr., skimming off foam frequently. Add remaining ingredients; cover and simmer 1 hr. Arrange meat and vegetables on a platter. Strain broth through cheesecloth; season to taste. *4 servings.*

BOUILLABAISSE

A Mediterranean specialty—the most famous and respected of all fish stews. To be truly authentic, a bouillabaisse should contain at least five different kinds of fish (not counting the shellfish). Our recipe is an American adaptation for your convenience and pleasure. This handsome dish is pictured opposite.

1 cup chopped onion	1 lb. cleaned raw shrimp, fresh or frozen*
¼ cup diced carrot	
1 clove garlic, minced	1 can (10 oz.) whole clams, undrained, or 1 doz. shell clams, shucked
½ cup olive or salad oil	
3 lb. frozen fish fillets (such as pike, haddock, or sole), thawed and cut into 3″ pieces	
	1 can (10½ oz.) beef broth
6 frozen lobster tails, thawed and cut in half*	½ cup chopped pimiento
	¼ cup chopped parsley
1 can (1 lb.) whole tomatoes	1 tbsp. salt
	1 tbsp. lemon juice
2 bay leaves, crushed	½ tsp. saffron
2 qt. water	Dash freshly ground pepper

In large kettle, cook and stir onion, carrot, and garlic in oil until onion is tender, about 10 min. Add fish fillets, lobster, tomatoes, bay leaves, and water. Heat to boiling; reduce heat. Cover and simmer gently 15 min. Add remaining ingredients; simmer gently 15 to 20 min. longer. *About 12 servings.*

*Bouillabaisse is more impressive than ever when the lobster and a few shrimp have been cooked in their shells.

TO SERVE FRENCH STYLE
Begin your bouillabaisse dinner with an hors d'oeuvres tray of fresh vegetables—perhaps tiny white-tipped radishes, celery, artichoke hearts, and chilled crisp-cooked asparagus spears.

When it's time for the main course, arrange all the fish in one dish and sprinkle with parsley. Strain the broth into a bowl containing slices of toasted garlic bread.

MULLIGATAWNY SOUP

Known for its popularity in England, this curry soup originated in the East Indies. ("Mulligatawny" means pepper water.) Various meats may be used; here is the more elegant chicken version.

3- to 4-lb. broiler-fryer chicken, cut up	1 stalk celery, sliced
1 qt. water	1 green pepper, diced
1 tbsp. salt	1 medium apple, pared and sliced
1 tsp. curry powder	¼ cup butter or margarine
⅛ tsp. mace	⅓ cup Gold Medal Flour (regular or Wondra)
⅛ tsp. cloves	
1 small bunch parsley	1 can (8 oz.) stewed tomatoes
1 medium onion, sliced	
1 medium carrot, sliced	

In large saucepan, combine chicken, water, and next 5 seasonings; cover and simmer 45 min., or until chicken is tender. Remove chicken from broth. Measure broth; if necessary, add water to make 1 qt. Remove bones and skin from chicken and cut meat into pieces. In large saucepan, cook and stir onion, carrot, celery, green pepper, and apple in butter until tender. Remove from heat; stir in flour. Gradually stir in broth and tomatoes. Add chicken. Heat to boiling, stirring constantly. Boil 1 min. Cover and simmer 1 hr. *8 to 10 servings.*

TO SERVE EAST INDIAN STYLE
Bring to the table in shallow soup plates, each topped with a spoonful of hot rice.

TO SERVE RUSSIAN STYLE
Ladle Borsch into large soup bowls. Top each with a spoonful of dairy sour cream, then sprinkle with freshly ground pepper. Pass rye bread for an accompaniment.

BORSCH

Hearty meat and vegetable soup beautifully colored with beets. See it pictured below.

1½ lb. shin bone	1 tsp. celery salt
1 lb. brisket or other soup meat, trimmed and cut into bite-size cubes	¼ tsp. crushed basil
	¼ tsp. paprika
	¼ tsp. pepper
2 to 3 tbsp. shortening	½ medium cabbage, finely shredded (about 2 cups)
4 cups water	
1 can (1 lb.) tomatoes	
1 cup chopped onion	1 large fresh beet, pared and diced (about 1 cup)
2 tbsp. minced parsley	
1½ tbsp. sugar	
1 clove garlic, minced	½ cup lemon juice (2 lemons)
½ bay leaf, crumbled	
2 tsp. salt	½ cup dairy sour cream

Cut any meat from shin bone into small chunks. Brown chunks and brisket in hot shortening in large kettle. Add bone, water, tomatoes, onion, and next 9 seasonings. Cover and simmer 1½ to 2 hr., or until meat is tender. Remove bone from soup and skim off excess fat. Add cabbage, beet, and lemon juice. Cover and cook 30 min. longer, or until vegetables are tender. (Additional water may be added, if necessary.) Top with sour cream. *10 servings.*

From Regional America—

Beloved traditional recipes shared
from north to south, east to west.

MANHATTAN CLAM CHOWDER

¼ cup finely cut bacon	1 cup water
¼ cup minced onion	⅓ cup diced celery
2 cans (7 oz. each) minced or whole clams*	1 can (1 lb.) tomatoes
2 cups diced pared potatoes	2 tsp. minced parsley
	1 tsp. salt
	¼ tsp. crushed thyme
	⅛ tsp. pepper

In large kettle, cook and stir bacon and onion until onion is tender. Drain clams, reserving liquor. Add clam liquor, potatoes, water, and celery to kettle. Simmer until potatoes are tender, about 15 min. Just before serving, add clams, tomatoes, and seasonings. Heat through. *6 servings.*

*Or use 1 pt. shucked fresh clams. Drain, reserving liquor. Chop clams and add with potatoes.

NEW ENGLAND CLAM CHOWDER

To complete your meal, pass oyster crackers and plan on a satisfying dessert of blueberry pie or cobbler.

¼ cup finely cut bacon or salt pork	2 cups diced pared potatoes
¼ cup minced onion	½ cup water
2 cans (7 oz. each) minced or whole clams*	2 cups milk
	1 tsp. salt
	⅛ tsp. pepper

In large kettle, cook and stir bacon and onion until onion is tender. Drain clams, reserving liquor. Add clam liquor, potatoes, and water to onion and bacon. Simmer until potatoes are tender, about 15 min. Just before serving, add clams, milk, salt, and pepper. Heat through. *6 servings.*

*Or use 1 pt. shucked fresh clams with liquor. Drain, reserving liquor. Chop clams and add with potatoes.

THE CHOWDER BATTLE

In the Northeast, clam chowder recipes are a matter of controversy. New Englanders claim it's an outrage to mix clams and tomatoes; New Yorkers, on the other hand, say chowder made with milk is only good for babies. Since to us both are delicious, we decline to take sides and have presented both here. Take your choice!

CHICKEN-SHRIMP GUMBO

Gumbo, a flavorful stew thickened with okra or filé powder, is a specialty of the Creole cuisine. Rich and thick, it's a wonderful meal in a dish!

4-lb. stewing hen, cut into serving-size pieces	1 tbsp. Worcestershire sauce
2 tsp. salt	1 tsp. salt
2 tbsp. shortening	1 tsp. crushed thyme
2½ cups cold water	¼ tsp. cayenne pepper
⅓ cup Gold Medal Flour (regular or Wondra)	2 bay leaves
2 cups chopped onion	1 clove garlic, minced
1 can (1 lb.) tomatoes	1 can (1 lb.) cut okra, drained
1 can (6 oz.) tomato paste	14 to 16 oz. cleaned raw shrimp, fresh or frozen
1 pkg. (10 oz.) frozen corn, broken apart	3 cups hot cooked rice
1 tbsp. sugar	

Sprinkle chicken pieces with 2 tsp. salt; brown well in hot shortening in large kettle. Remove chicken from kettle and drain on paper towels. Drain fat from kettle. Mix water and flour; pour into kettle. Heat to boiling, stirring constantly. Stir in onion, tomatoes, tomato paste, corn, sugar, Worcestershire sauce, 1 tsp. salt, the thyme, cayenne pepper, bay leaves, and garlic; add chicken. Cover and simmer 2 hr. Stir occasionally and skim off excess fat. Add okra and simmer uncovered until chicken is tender, about 1 hr. Add shrimp and cook 10 to 20 min., or until shrimp is pink. Do not overcook shrimp. Remove from heat. Lift out bay leaves. (If desired, add ¼ tsp. gumbo filé powder to each bowl; stir well. Gumbo filé powder will thicken mixture slightly.) To serve, place a scoop of rice in each soup plate. Fill with gumbo; then add a piece of chicken. *8 to 10 servings.*

Betty Crocker Note: Frozen shrimp may have a glaze over it; rinse off before adding to soup or mixture will become too thin.

EASY CHICKEN GUMBO

1 can (1 lb.) cut okra, drained	1 can (1 lb.) tomatoes
¼ cup chopped onion	1 small bay leaf
¼ cup chopped green pepper	Salt and pepper
3 tbsp. butter or margarine	1 cup diced cooked chicken
4 cups consommé or chicken broth*	1 tbsp. minced parsley
	3 cups hot cooked rice

In large saucepan, cook and stir okra, onion, and green pepper in butter over low heat until onion is tender. Stir in consommé, tomatoes, and bay leaf; simmer 15 min. Season to taste with salt and pepper. Stir in chicken and parsley; heat through. Serve in bowls with scoops of rice. *6 servings.*

*Chicken broth may be made by dissolving 4 chicken bouillon cubes in 4 cups boiling water, or use canned chicken broth.

FILÉ POWDER

The early gumbos of the New Orleans Creole cuisine were flavored with filé powder, a favorite seasoning with good Southern cooks. Made of young, tender sassafras leaves, filé powder was a specialty of the Choctaw Indians, who gathered the leaves, pounded them finely and sold the powder in the French Market of the city. A seasoning that serves also to thicken, filé powder should be added only after the gumbo is taken from the heat to avoid lumps.

Its distinctive flavor is still a necessary ingredient in the opinion of many classic gumbo fanciers, and it may be found bottled on many grocers' spice shelves and in specialty food shops. Descendants of the Choctaws still prepare it for market.

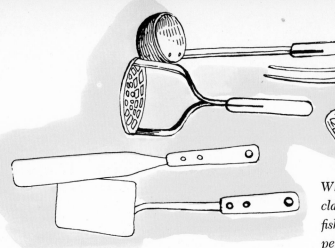

KENTUCKY BURGOO

Kentucky pioneers found recreation and excitement in burgoo feasts. Variations of this appetizing concoction of beef, veal, chicken, and vegetables are now served throughout the country, especially on May 1, Derby Day.

4- to 5-lb. stewing hen, cut up
1 lb. stewing beef, cut into 2″ pieces
1 lb. veal shoulder, cut into 2″ pieces
6 small potatoes, pared and halved (1 lb.)
6 small onions, halved (1 lb.)
3 cups chopped celery
2 cups sliced carrots
2 medium green peppers, chopped
1 pkg. (10 oz.) frozen Lima beans, broken apart
1 can (1 lb.) cut okra, diced, or 1 pkg. (10 oz.) frozen okra, broken apart
1 can (1 lb.) whole kernel corn
1 can (1 lb.) tomatoes
1 can (10½ oz.) tomato pureé
2 tbsp. salt
1½ tsp. dry mustard
1 tsp. pepper
1 tsp. chili powder
¼ tsp. Tabasco
⅛ tsp. cayenne pepper
½ cup minced parsley

Place chicken and meat in large heavy kettle. Add water just to cover meat (2½ to 3 qt.). Cover and cook over low heat until tender, 2 to 3 hr. Remove meat; skim off excess fat. Remove skin from chicken; bone and cut up chicken meat. Return chicken, beef, and veal to broth in kettle; add remaining ingredients except parsley. Simmer uncovered until flavors are blended, 2½ to 3 hr. Just before serving, stir in parsley. *15 to 20 servings.*

CIOPPINO

When it comes to soups, Cioppino is San Francisco's claim to fame! The original recipe calls for both fish and shellfish. Our version is a simpler, less expensive one—ideal for Friday night suppers. Serve with hot garlic bread or Parmesan toast.

⅔ cup chopped onion
2 small carrots, sliced
2 tbsp. minced parsley
1 clove garlic, minced
¼ cup salad oil
2 tbsp. flour
½ tsp. salt
¼ tsp. pepper
1 can (15 oz.) tomato sauce
2 cups hot water
1½ lb. fresh halibut or 2 pkg. (12 oz. each) frozen halibut, thawed

In large skillet, cook and stir onion, carrots, parsley, and garlic in hot oil until onion is tender. Remove from heat. Stir in flour, salt, and pepper. Cook over low heat, stirring until mixture is bubbly. Remove from heat. Stir in tomato sauce and water. Cover; simmer 20 min. Remove bones and skin from fish; cut into 1″ cubes; add to sauce. Cover; simmer 30 to 40 min. *6 servings.*

CHILI CONCOCTION

Hot and hearty, typical of the Southwest.

2 lb. ground beef
2 cups chopped onions
2 cans (1 lb. 12 oz. each) tomatoes
1 can (8 oz.) tomato sauce
2 cans (1 lb. each) kidney beans, drained (reserve liquid)
1 tbsp. sugar
1½ to 2 tbsp. chili powder
2 tsp. salt

Brown meat and onions in large kettle. Stir in tomatoes, tomato sauce, liquid from kidney beans, and seasonings. Simmer uncovered 45 min, stirring occasionally. Stir in beans and simmer 15 min., or until of desired consistency. *6 to 8 servings.*

From the Good Old Days—*Recipes handed down from mother to daughter.*

OLD-FASHIONED BEEF STEW

½ cup Gold Medal Flour
  (regular or Wondra)
½ tsp. paprika
¼ tsp. pepper
2 lb. chuck or bottom
  round, cut into 2″
  pieces
1 tbsp. shortening
1 qt. hot water

3 pared potatoes, cubed
1 medium turnip, cubed
4 carrots, quartered
1 cup diced celery
½ cup diced parsnips
1 green pepper, cut into
  strips
½ cup diced onion
2 tsp. salt
2 beef bouillon cubes

Mix flour, paprika, and the pepper; roll meat in flour mixture. Brown thoroughly in hot shortening. Add water; simmer covered 2 hr. (Add more water, if necessary.) Add remaining ingredients. Cook until vegetables are tender, about 30 min. *8 servings.*

OXTAIL STEW

2 lb. disjointed oxtails
¼ cup Gold Medal Flour
  (regular or Wondra)
1 tsp. salt
¼ cup shortening
1 cup tomato juice
½ cup water
1 tsp. salt

4 whole allspice
1 bay leaf, crumbled
1 clove garlic, minced
1 cup chopped onion
4 carrots, quartered
4 small onions, peeled
2 tbsp. lemon juice

Rinse oxtails in cold water; drain. Mix flour and 1 tsp. salt; roll meat in flour mixture. Brown in hot shortening. Add tomato juice, water, seasonings, and chopped onion. Cover and simmer 2½ hr. Skim off excess fat, if necessary. Add carrots, whole onions, and lemon juice; cover and simmer 45 min., or until vegetables are tender. *4 servings.*

MEATBALL STEW AND PARSLEY DUMPLINGS

1 lb. ground beef	½ cup water
½ lb. ground fresh pork	2 tbsp. shortening
2 tbsp. instant minced onion	¼ cup hot water
¾ cup dry bread crumbs	2 tbsp. Bisquick
1 tbsp. minced parsley	½ tsp. salt
1½ tsp. salt	¼ tsp. each paprika and pepper
⅛ tsp. pepper	2 cups boiling water
1½ tsp. Worcestershire sauce	Parsley Dumplings (below)
1 egg	¾ cup dairy sour cream

Mix meats, onion, bread crumbs, parsley, 1½ tsp. salt, ⅛ tsp. pepper, the Worcestershire sauce, egg, and ½ cup water. Form mixture into small balls. Brown in hot shortening; add ¼ cup water and simmer 10 min. Remove meatballs. Blend Bisquick, ½ tsp. salt, the paprika, and pepper into the fat in skillet; stir in the boiling water. Heat to boiling, stirring constantly; add meatballs.

Drop Parsley Dumplings by spoonfuls onto hot stew. Cook uncovered over low heat 10 min.; cover and cook 10 min. longer. (Liquid should just bubble gently.) Remove dumplings. Stir in sour cream and heat just to boiling. Serve immediately. *6 servings.*

PARSLEY DUMPLINGS

With a fork, thoroughly mix 2 cups Bisquick, ¾ cup milk, and ¼ cup minced parsley.

VEAL STEW WITH CORNMEAL DUMPLINGS

2 medium slices salt pork	Dash pepper
1½ lb. veal stew meat, cut into 1″ cubes	1 cup diced pared potatoes
4 cups tomato juice	½ cup diced celery
1 tsp. salt	½ cup chopped onion
2 to 3 dashes Tabasco	Cornmeal Dumplings (below)

Fry salt pork in Dutch oven or large skillet until crisp; remove pork and set aside. Brown veal slowly in pork fat over medium-low heat, about 30 min. Drain off excess fat. Crumble salt pork and add to veal with tomato juice and seasonings. Cover and simmer 1 hr. (do not boil). Add potatoes, celery, and onion; cover and simmer 30 min. longer, or until vegetables are almost tender. (If necessary, add ½ to 1 cup tomato juice.) Drop rounded tablespoonfuls of Cornmeal Dumplings onto hot stew. Cook uncovered over low heat 10 min.; cover and cook 10 min. longer. (Liquid should just bubble gently.) Serve immediately. *6 to 8 servings.*

CORNMEAL DUMPLINGS

Stir together 1½ cups Bisquick, ½ cup yellow cornmeal, and 2 tsp. parsley flakes. Add ¾ cup milk all at once and mix well with a fork.

Pictured: Old-fashioned Beef Stew

SPRINGTIME SKILLET STEW

Lamb, potatoes, and bright green peas simmer in herb-flavored bouillon. For a go-along treat, pass Surprise Minted Muffins.

1½ lb. lamb shoulder, cut into 2″ cubes	½ tsp. salt
1 tbsp. shortening	¼ tsp. celery seed
2 medium onions, chopped	¼ tsp. crushed marjoram
2 cups beef bouillon*	⅛ tsp. crushed thyme
3 medium potatoes, pared and thinly sliced	¼ tsp. pepper
	1 pkg. (10 oz.) frozen green peas, broken apart

In large skillet, brown meat well in hot shortening. Drain off excess fat. Add onions; cook and stir until tender. Pour bouillon over meat and onions; cover and simmer 2 hr. Stir in potatoes and seasonings. Simmer covered 30 min. longer. Skim off excess fat. Stir in peas; cook covered 10 min. *4 servings.*

*Beef bouillon may be made by dissolving 2 beef bouillon cubes in 2 cups boiling water, or use canned beef broth.

MINTED MUFFINS ARE A SURPRISE

The mint jelly hides inside. Follow directions for muffins on package of Bisquick except—fill muffin cups only ⅓ full of batter, then drop ½ tsp. mint jelly in center. Add more batter to fill cup ⅔ full.

VEGETABLE SOUP

1 soup bone with meat	1 cup sliced celery and leaves
2 tbsp. shortening	1 can (1 lb.) tomatoes
4 cups hot water	3 sprigs parsley, finely cut
½ bay leaf	1 tbsp. salt
3 peppercorns	¼ tsp. crushed marjoram
1 medium onion, chopped	¼ tsp. crushed thyme
1 cup sliced carrots	

Cut meat off soup bone; cut into small chunks. Brown in hot shortening in large kettle. Add water and bone; cover and simmer 1½ to 2 hr. Remove bone and skim fat from top of soup. Place bay leaf and peppercorns in tea ball or tie in cheesecloth bag; add to soup. Add remaining ingredients; cook 20 to 30 min. longer, or until vegetables are tender. Remove tea ball or cheesecloth bag. *6 to 8 servings.*

STORMY DAY BEAN SOUP

Add just one more hearty food to this supper—squares of warm corn bread or cherry pie for dessert. For salad, serve crisp tossed greens.

1 lb. dry navy beans	2 qt. water
1 ham bone	½ tsp. salt
2 cups cubed ham	Dash pepper
1 small onion, finely chopped	1 bay leaf

Rinse beans. Soak 3 hr.; drain. In large kettle, combine all ingredients; heat to boiling. Cover; simmer 3 hr., or until beans are tender. (Add more water, if necessary.) Skim off foam occasionally. Before serving, remove bay leaf and ham bone. Trim meat from bone; add to soup. Salt to taste. *6 to 8 servings.*

SIMMERED AND SAVORY —ON THE DOUBLE

EASY CORN-CLAM CHOWDER

1 can (10 oz.) frozen
  clam chowder
1 can (7 oz.) whole
  kernel corn
1 tsp. onion flakes
¼ tsp. salt
⅛ tsp. pepper

Prepare clam chowder as directed on can except—stir in corn (with liquid) and seasonings. Sprinkle with paprika or minced parsley, if desired. *3 servings.*

CHEESE CHOWDER

1 pkg. (10 oz.) frozen
  mixed vegetables,
  cooked and drained
1 can (10½ oz.) cream of
  chicken soup
1 soup can milk
1 cup shredded Cheddar
  cheese

Combine vegetables, soup, and milk in saucepan. Heat to simmering, stirring occasionally. Sprinkle with cheese. *4 servings.*

BEEF TUREEN

A "quickie" for a hurried-but-hearty family dinner.

1 can (1 lb.) tomatoes,
  drained (reserve liquid)
¾ tsp. celery seed
½ tsp. salt
¼ tsp. pepper
⅛ tsp. garlic powder
1 pkg. (10 oz.) frozen
  mixed vegetables
1 can (1½ lb.) beef stew

Add enough water to reserved tomato liquid to make 1 cup; pour into saucepan. Stir in seasonings. Heat to boiling. Add mixed vegetables; return to boiling, separating vegetables with fork. Cover and simmer 8 min., or until vegetables are crisp tender. Stir in stew and drained tomatoes; heat through. *4 to 6 servings.*

CRABMEAT SOUP (Mongole)

This makes an elegant party soup served in cups or mugs with rye melba toast.

1 can (11¼ oz.) green
  pea soup
1 can (10½ oz.) tomato
  soup
2 soup cans milk
½ cup light cream
¼ cup sherry
1 can (6½ oz.) crabmeat,
  drained and cartilage
  removed

Combine soups in saucepan. Gradually stir in milk. Add cream, sherry, and crabmeat. Heat slowly, stirring occasionally (do not boil). *6 servings.*

FRANK AND TATER SOUP

8 bacon slices, cut into
  small pieces
4 frankfurters or 4 oz.
  pepperoni, thinly
  sliced and quartered
½ cup chopped onion
1 can (13¾ oz.) chicken
  broth
1 tsp. celery salt
1 pkg. of our mashed
  Potato Buds
1 can (1 lb.) whole
  kernel corn
1⅔ cups milk

In medium saucepan, cook bacon and frankfurters until bacon is crisp. Spoon off 2 tbsp. fat. Add onion; cook over low heat until onion is tender. Add broth and celery salt. Heat to boiling; remove from heat. Measure amount of mashed Potato Buds as directed on package for 4 servings. Stir measured potatoes into soup. Stir in corn (with liquid) and milk. Heat through; season with salt, if desired. *4 to 6 servings.*

CREAM OF AVOCADO SOUP

Pictured at left.

¾ cup milk	⅛ tsp. salt
1 can (10½ oz.) cream of chicken soup	Dash pepper
	Dash nutmeg
1 can (6½ oz.) white tuna, well drained	1 ripe avocado
	4 slices lemon
⅛ tsp. grated lemon peel	

Stir together milk, soup, tuna, lemon peel, and seasonings in saucepan; heat through. Peel avocado; remove seed. Shred avocado; stir into soup; heat. Pour into serving bowls; garnish with lemon slices. *4 servings.*

QUICK VEGETABLE SOUP WITH FRANK SLICES

2 cans (10½ oz. each) beef broth	3 carrots, cut into julienne strips
1 soup can water	2 small onions, thinly sliced
2 cloves garlic, minced	
2 tbsp. butter	6 frankfurters, each cut crosswise into 4 pieces
1½ tsp. crushed basil	
1 tsp. monosodium glutamate	1 lb. zucchini squash, cut into ¼″ slices
1 tsp. salt	3 tomatoes, peeled and cut into eighths
⅛ tsp. pepper	

In large saucepan, combine all ingredients except frankfurters, zucchini, and tomatoes. Cover and simmer 20 min. Add remaining ingredients. Heat to boiling; cover and simmer 10 min. *6 servings.*

SOUTH-OF-THE-BORDER SOUP

A thick, hearty chili stew. Pictured at left.

1 can (10½ oz.) bean with bacon soup	1 soup can water
	⅛ to ¼ tsp. garlic powder
1 can (10½ oz.) tomato soup	Corn chips
1 can (10½ oz.) chili without beans	

Stir soups, water, and garlic powder in saucepan. Heat to boiling. Ladle soup into bowls; top with corn chips. *4 to 6 servings.*

Planned-overs

Here is proof that you never can have too much of a good thing—of meat or poultry, broth or gravy. Making an "all-new" meal in a dish from Sunday's roast or last night's party chicken is easy, inexpensive, and fun when you take an imaginative look at the whole week's menus and plan ahead as you shop.

Buy a larger-than-necessary roast (it will be juicier and more flavorful than a smaller cut), a whole ham or leg of lamb rather than half, two chickens instead of just one. Cook your purchase all at one time and serve it grandly for a fine, full-dress dinner. Next day, or later in the week, follow one of these "planned-over" recipes. You'll find this is the way to simplify shopping, balance your food budget, save cooking time and fuel, *and* feed your family with flair.

Bake a Big Beautiful Ham and *then:*

HAM 'N CORN BREAD BAKE

1½ cups cubed cooked ham
1 cup drained cooked Lima beans
1 can (8 oz.) cream style corn
1 cup shredded sharp Cheddar cheese
½ cup milk
2 tbsp. minced onion
1 tsp. Worcestershire sauce
Corn Bread Topping (below)

Heat oven to 400°. Mix all ingredients except Corn Bread Topping. Pour into greased 1½-qt. casserole. Cover; bake 15 min., or until bubbly at edges. Prepare Corn Bread Topping; pour over hot mixture, spreading evenly to edges. Bake uncovered 20 min. longer. Cut into wedges with spatula; turn out upside down onto plate. Garnish with parsley, if desired. *4 servings.*

CORN BREAD TOPPING

⅔ cup Bisquick
⅓ cup cornmeal
1 tbsp. sugar
1 egg
⅓ cup milk

Mix all ingredients; beat vigorously 30 seconds.

CORN AND HAM FRITTERS

1¼ cups Gold Medal Flour (regular or Wondra)
2 tsp. baking powder
½ tsp. celery salt
½ tsp. paprika
2 egg yolks
¼ cup milk
1 tsp. grated onion
1 cup chopped cooked ham
1 can (8¾ oz.) cream style corn
2 egg whites, stiffly beaten
Orange Sauce (below)

Stir together dry ingredients. Beat egg yolks with milk; stir into dry ingredients until moistened. Add onion, ham, and corn. Fold in egg whites. Heat fat to 375° (a 1″ cube of bread browns in 60 seconds). Drop tablespoonfuls of batter into hot fat. Fry 4 to 6 min. Fritters will be quite brown. Remove from fat; drain on rack over paper towels. Sprinkle with confectioners' sugar, if desired. Serve with Orange Sauce or syrup. *4 servings (about sixteen 2″ fritters).*

ORANGE SAUCE

3 tbsp. flour
⅓ cup sugar
¼ tsp. salt
¼ tsp. dry mustard
1 cup water
⅓ cup orange juice
1 tbsp. butter or margarine

Stir together dry ingredients. Gradually stir in water. Bring to boiling, stirring constantly. Boil 1 min. Remove from heat. Stir in orange juice and butter. *Makes about 1¼ cups sauce.*

Roast an Extra Pound or Two of Pork and *then:*

CHINESE PORK AND FRIED RICE

⅔ cup uncooked regular
  rice
1 medium onion, chopped
2 stalks celery, sliced
  diagonally
2 tbsp. salad oil

1½ cups boiling water
1 beef or chicken
  bouillon cube
2 tbsp. soy sauce
1½ cups diced cooked
  pork
1 green pepper, chopped

Cook and stir rice, onion, and celery in hot oil until rice is golden brown and onion is tender. Stir in remaining ingredients except green pepper; heat to boiling. Lower heat; cover tightly and simmer 15 to 18 min., or until rice is tender and liquid is absorbed. Remove from heat; add green pepper and fluff rice lightly with fork. Cover for 10 min. Serve with additional soy sauce, if desired. *3 or 4 servings.*

DEVILED PORK BURGERS

8 thin slices cooked
  roast pork
¾ cup bottled barbecue
  sauce

4 sesame hamburger
  buns, split in half
Butter or margarine
4 slices onion
4 green pepper rings

Combine pork and barbecue sauce in saucepan. Simmer uncovered 10 min., stirring occasionally. Butter buns; place cut side up on broiler rack. Place one onion slice surrounded with a green pepper ring on top half of each bun. Set oven control at "broil." Broil buns 4 to 5″ from source of heat until bread is golden brown. To serve, place 2 meat slices on bottom half of each bun; spoon sauce over meat. *4 servings.*

MORE "PLANNED-OVER" HAM OR PORK RECIPES

All-in-One Salad (p. 126)
Cheese-Potato Salad with Julienne Ham (p. 128)
Chef's Salad (p. 124)
Curried Noodles Romanoff (p. 60)
Four-layer Dinner (p. 62)
Fruited Baked Squash (p. 94)
Golden Gate Casserole (p. 62)
Ham 'n Cabbage Quickie (p. 69)
Stuffed Peppers Festivo (p. 94)
Summer Salad Bowl (p. 127)
Sunny Mustard Mousse with Ham Salad (p. 130)

Roast an Extra Pound or Two of Beef and *then:*

CRISPY BROWNED HASH

1 cup chopped cooked beef
1 cup chopped cooked
   potatoes
1 onion, chopped

1 tbsp. minced parsley
Salt and pepper to taste
1 to 2 tbsp. shortening
½ cup milk

Combine all ingredients except shortening and milk. Heat shortening in heavy skillet over medium heat. When shortening is very hot, spread hash evenly in skillet. Brown hash quickly, 10 to 15 min. Add milk and mix. Cover and cook slowly about 10 min., or until crisp. *2 to 3 servings.*

MORE "PLANNED-OVER" BEEF OR VEAL RECIPES

Chef's Salad (p. 124)
Hot Beef Sandwiches (p. 135)

GILDED POT ROAST

3 carrots, cut into
   julienne strips
2 parsnips, cut into
   julienne strips
6 to 8 slices cooked
   roast beef
1 cup beef gravy

2 cups seasoned mashed
   potatoes
1 tbsp. instant minced
   onion
1 tbsp. chopped chives
2 tsp. prepared mustard
2 tbsp. grated Parmesan
   cheese

Heat oven to 350°. Cook the carrots and parsnips covered in 1″ boiling salted water until tender; drain. Overlap meat slices in square baking dish, 8x8x2″. Pour gravy over meat. Mix potatoes with onion, chives, and mustard. Drop spoonfuls of potato mixture around edge of dish. Place carrots and parsnips in center; sprinkle with Parmesan cheese. Bake uncovered 30 min., or until gravy is bubbly. *4 to 6 servings.*

VEAL PATTIES PARMIGIANO

1½ cups finely chopped
   or ground cooked veal
½ cup grated Parmesan
   cheese
¼ cup milk
2 tbsp. crushed cracker
   crumbs
1 egg

3 tbsp. salad oil
1 pkg. (1½ to 2½ oz.) dry
   spaghetti sauce mix*
4 to 8 slices mozzarella
   cheese
7 to 8 oz. spaghetti,
   cooked and drained

Thoroughly mix veal, Parmesan cheese, milk, cracker crumbs, and egg; shape mixture into 4 patties. Thoroughly brown one side of patties in hot oil; turn carefully and brown other side. Drain patties on paper towels. Drain fat from skillet. In same skillet, prepare spaghetti sauce mix and simmer as directed on package. Add meat patties, spooning sauce over them. Cover and simmer 5 min. Top each patty with 1 or 2 slices mozzarella cheese; cover and simmer 5 min. longer, or until cheese melts. Serve over hot cooked spaghetti. *4 servings.*

*Check package directions to see if the mix you have selected requires the addition of canned tomato sauce or paste.

Roast an Extra Pound or Two of Lamb and *then:*

SHEPHERDS' PIE

Quickie version of a famous English country dish.

1 pkg. of our mashed
  Potato Buds
2 cups cubed cooked
  lamb
¼ cup chopped onion

2 cups cooked vegetables
  (carrots, peas, or corn)
2 cans (10¾ oz. each)
  mushroom gravy
½ tsp. salt

Heat oven to 350°. Prepare our mashed Potato Buds as directed on package for 4 servings; set aside. In large bowl, mix remaining ingredients; pour into 2-qt. casserole. Mound potatoes in a ring around edge of dish. Bake 30 min., or until potatoes are slightly browned. *4 to 6 servings.*

GREEK GODDESS SALAD

Gloriously seasoned with herbs, lemon juice, and olive oil, this marinated lamb salad is a delight!

1 eggplant
Lemon juice
1 tsp. salt
1 tsp. crushed oregano
¼ tsp. garlic salt
½ cup olive oil
2 cups cubed cooked
  lamb
1 cup minced parsley
1 cup chopped celery

¼ cup sliced green onion
2 tomatoes, cut into
  eighths
1 tbsp. sugar
2 tbsp. lemon juice
2 tbsp. tarragon vinegar
1 tsp. crushed mint leaves
Freshly ground black
  pepper

Cut eggplant in half lengthwise. Scoop out pulp; dice. Brush inside of eggplant shells with lemon juice to prevent discoloration. Cook and stir diced eggplant, salt, oregano, and garlic salt in hot oil until eggplant is tender. Remove to large bowl; add lamb, parsley, celery, green onion, and tomatoes. Mix sugar, 2 tbsp. lemon juice, the vinegar, mint, and pepper. Pour over ingredients in bowl; toss lightly. Cover and chill at least 2 hr., stirring gently once or twice. Just before serving, toss salad lightly. Fill eggplant shells with chilled salad. *4 servings.*

FLAVORSOME CABBAGE ROLLS

8 large cabbage leaves
1 can (8 oz.) tomato
  sauce with mushrooms
2 cups coarsely chopped
  cooked lamb
½ cup uncooked regular
  rice
½ cup finely chopped
  onion

2 tbsp. lemon juice
2 tsp. Worcestershire
  sauce
1 clove garlic, minced
¼ cup water
¼ cup beef broth*
2 tbsp. cornstarch
1½ cups beef broth*
1 tbsp. chopped chives

Place cabbage leaves in boiling salted water; simmer gently 3 min. Drain and cool slightly. Reserve 2 tbsp. tomato sauce. Mix remaining sauce with lamb, rice, onion, lemon juice, Worcestershire sauce, garlic, and water. Place an eighth of this mixture in the center of each cabbage leaf; roll up. Place rolls, seam side down, in skillet with ¼ cup beef broth. Cover; simmer 45 min. (Add more beef broth, if necessary.) Mix cornstarch, reserved tomato sauce, 1½ cups beef broth, and the chives. Remove cabbage rolls to heated serving plate. Stir cornstarch mixture into skillet. Heat to boiling, stirring constantly; boil 1 min. Pour over rolls or serve as an accompanying sauce. *4 servings.*

*Beef broth may be made by dissolving 2 beef bouillon cubes in 1¾ cups boiling water, or use canned beef broth.

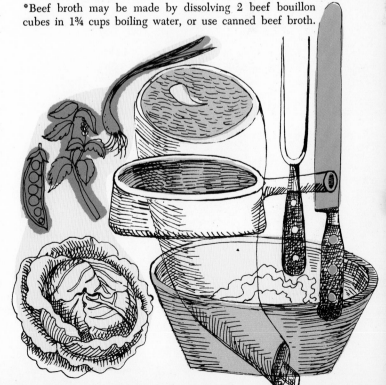

Cook Two Chickens or a Large Turkey and *then:*

POTATO PUFF

Pictured opposite.

1 pkg. of our mashed
  Potato Buds
1 cup shredded sharp
  Cheddar cheese (4 oz.)
1 cup finely chopped
  cooked chicken or
  turkey
1 cup shredded carrots
  (2 to 3)
2 tsp. chopped chives
Pinch crushed rosemary
3 egg yolks, slightly
  beaten
3 egg whites
½ tsp. salt

Heat oven to 350°. Prepare potatoes as directed on package for 4 servings. Stir in cheese, chicken, carrots, herbs, and egg yolks. Beat egg whites and salt until stiff peaks form; fold into potato mixture. Pour into buttered 2-qt. casserole; place casserole in pan of hot water (1″ deep). Bake uncovered 50 to 60 min., or until browned and puffed. *4 servings.*

CHICKEN CARUSO

Red pimiento, green peas, and chunks of good meat from the Christmas bird—now here's a colorful and delicious dish for holiday entertaining!

8 oz. uncooked elbow
  macaroni
4 cups chicken broth*
2 slices bacon, cut up
½ cup finely chopped
  green pepper
⅓ cup finely chopped
  onion
2 cups cubed cooked
  chicken or turkey
1 pkg. (10 oz.) frozen
  green peas, cooked
  and drained
2 cups shredded process
  American cheese
¼ cup chopped pimiento
¼ cup toasted slivered
  almonds
3 tbsp. sherry

Boil macaroni in chicken broth 10 min., or until tender; do not drain. Fry bacon until crisp in large heavy skillet. Add green pepper and onion; cook and stir until onion is just tender. Drain off excess fat. Add macaroni (with broth) and remaining ingredients; stir to mix. Heat through. Garnish with tomato slices and parsley, if desired. *6 to 8 servings.*

*Chicken broth may be made by dissolving 4 chicken bouillon cubes in 4 cups boiling water, or use canned chicken broth.

TURKEY IN STUFFING SHELLS

Pictured opposite.

1½ tbsp. flour
1 tsp. instant minced
  onion
¼ tsp. salt
¼ tsp. mace
Freshly ground black
  pepper
1¼ cups light cream
2 cups cubed cooked
  turkey or chicken
1 pkg. (10 oz.) frozen
  green peas with onions,
  cooked and drained
2 tbsp. chopped pimiento
1 tsp. grated lemon peel
Stuffing Shells (below)

Heat oven to 425°. Combine flour, onion, and seasonings in heavy saucepan. Gradually stir in cream. Heat to boiling, stirring constantly. Boil 1 min. Stir in turkey, peas with onions, pimiento, and lemon peel; heat through. Pour hot mixture into Stuffing Shells. Sprinkle reserved stuffing mixture around edge of each dish. Bake 5 min., or until stuffing edge is lightly browned. *5 servings.*

STUFFING SHELLS

2 cups crushed packaged
  herb-seasoned stuffing
⅓ cup butter or margarine,
  melted
¼ cup water

Toss stuffing with the butter and water. Reserve 1¼ cups for crumb border. Divide remaining stuffing mixture among five 6-inch pie pans or individual casseroles; press mixture to bottom and sides of each casserole.

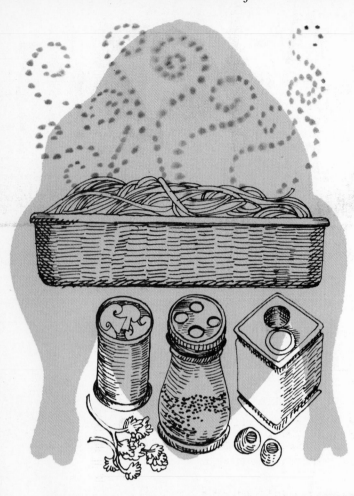

CHICKEN TETRAZZINI

¼ cup butter
¼ cup Gold Medal Flour
   (regular or Wondra)
½ tsp. salt
¼ tsp. pepper
1 cup chicken broth*
1 cup whipping cream
2 tbsp. sherry

7 oz. spaghetti, broken
   into small pieces,
   cooked and drained
2 cups cubed cooked
   chicken or turkey
1 can (3 oz.) sliced
   mushrooms, drained
½ cup grated Parmesan
   cheese

Heat oven to 350°. Melt butter over low heat. Blend in flour and seasonings. Cook, stirring until mixture is smooth and bubbly. Remove from heat. Stir in broth and cream. Heat to boiling, stirring constantly. Boil 1 min. Add sherry. Stir in spaghetti, chicken, and mushrooms. Pour into a square baking dish, 8x8x2″. Sprinkle with Parmesan cheese. Bake 30 min., or until bubbly in center. If desired, brown top by placing briefly under broiler. Garnish with parsley and green olives, if desired. *6 servings.*

*Chicken broth may be made by dissolving 1 chicken bouillon cube in 1 cup boiling water, or use canned chicken broth.

MORE "PLANNED-OVER" CHICKEN OR TURKEY RECIPES

Salads & Sandwiches that Satisfy

Cornucopias of plenty—these salad meals and sandwich plates are filled to over-flowing with appealing fresh flavors. True meals in a dish, they are hearty with meat or fowl or seafood, crisp with garden greens, tangy with delicious dressings. Each can be the mainstay of many a meal, from a substantial lunch to a Sunday evening or midnight supper.

You'll want to serve a salad or sandwich supper for the change of pace it offers, or just to match the weather or your casual mood of the day. Begin with soup, then pass a hot bread or toasted crackers with the salad or crunchy relishes with the sandwich course. Finish with a dessert as simple as ice-cream sundaes or as filling as warm homemade apple pie.

Main-dish Salads

A one-dish dinner from the following pages is really salad and entrée in one! Planned to charm the eye and tempt the taste, these salad meals are delightful combinations of texture and flavor. To add an extra loving touch, be sure to pass a basket heaped with hot breads.

On warm summer days that call for cool cooking—or perhaps, no cooking—see how a jellied seafood mold, chef's salad, or a platter of chilled vegetables vinaigrette will rouse the most languishing appetite. And as the seasons change, introduce the fresh fruits and vegetables to your table in these salads; when fall and winter arrive, sometimes serve a zesty steaming salad hot from the oven.

SALAD SENTIMENTS

- Serve chilled salads directly from the refrigerator; hot (oven) salads right from the oven.
- Drain fruits and vegetables well before adding to the salad bowl.
- Cut each ingredient into bite-size pieces—try for a variety of colors, shapes, and flavors.
- To add flavor to meat, fowl, or seafood, marinate (let stand) in a marinade (mixture of oil, salt, vinegar or lemon juice, and seasonings) for one or two hours before adding to the salad.
- To cook chicken, turkey, or shrimp, see success tips on pages 143 and 144.
- Use freshly ground pepper from your pepper grinder.
- Buy two or more kinds of greens for light and dark color contrast and for variety in flavor and leaf shape. To remove leaves from head lettuce, core and fill cavity with cold running water; turn upside down to drain. (Note: To core easily and with a minimum of waste, strike lettuce head sharply, core side down, on counter edge to loosen. Remove core with fingers.) Wash other greens in generous amounts of cool water, discarding wilted or discolored leaves. Swing dry in French wire salad basket or pat dry with clean towels. Store in refrigerator in a pliofilm bag or in hydrator.
- Tear—do not cut—salad greens into bite-size pieces.

- Toss greens with dressing just before serving. (Note: If salad must stand in dressing while being served at a buffet, place an inverted saucer in bottom of bowl to trap excess dressing. Leave saucer in place while serving.)
- To make a molded salad, prepare gelatin base as directed in recipe. Chill until slightly thickened. Fold in solid ingredients. Turn into mold and chill until firm, about 3 to 4 hr.

SALAD DRESSINGS

A good dressing should be made shortly before serving and allowed to chill for about 30 minutes to develop and blend the flavors. Olive, peanut, safflower, or other salad oils may be used in French dressing. A wine or herb vinegar will add subtle bouquet and authority to the dressing.

FRENCH DRESSING

1 cup olive oil, salad oil, or combination	1 tsp. salt
¼ cup vinegar	½ tsp. dry mustard
¼ cup lemon juice	½ tsp. paprika

Beat all ingredients with rotary beater or shake well in tightly covered jar. Keep in covered jar in refrigerator. Shake again to mix before using. *Makes 1 ½ cups.*

PATIO BUFFET PLATTER

Marinated Vegetables
(below)

Stuffed Tomatoes
(right)

Blue Cheese Balls
(right)

2 cups raw cauliflowerets

Crisp lettuce leaves

Prepare Marinated Vegetables, Stuffed Tomatoes, and Blue Cheese Balls. Arrange with cauliflowerets on a large platter. *4 servings.*

MARINATED VEGETABLES

4 medium carrots, cut into julienne strips, cooked and drained

1 pkg. (10 oz.) frozen Lima beans, cooked and drained

1 can (4 oz.) button mushrooms, drained

¼ cup wine vinegar

2 tbsp. water

½ envelope Italian salad-dressing mix

½ envelope onion salad-dressing mix

⅔ cup salad oil or olive oil

Arrange carrots, Lima beans, and mushrooms in separate sections in oblong baking dish, 10x6x1½". In a cruet or tightly covered jar, shake together vinegar, water, and salad dressing mixes. Add oil and shake again. Pour dressing over vegetables; cover. Chill at least 2 hr., or overnight, turning vegetables occasionally. When ready to serve, use a slotted spoon to place vegetables on platter.

Note: Leftover dressing may be stored in a tightly covered jar for later use.

STUFFED TOMATOES

3 hard-cooked eggs, chopped

½ medium cucumber, chopped

¼ cup chopped green pepper

2 tbsp. chopped green onion

¼ cup salad dressing or mayonnaise

4 chilled tomatoes, peeled

Salt

Cucumber slices

Combine eggs, cucumber, green pepper, onion, and salad dressing; chill. Cut tomatoes lengthwise into 6 sections, not quite cutting through. Pull wedges apart slightly. Sprinkle with salt. Spoon egg salad into center of tomatoes. Place cucumber slices between tomato sections.

BLUE CHEESE BALLS

Blend 1 cup crumbled blue cheese with 2 tbsp. light cream. Form into walnut-size balls; roll in snipped parsley. Chill.

CHEF'S SALAD

1 head lettuce
½ bunch romaine or
    endive
½ cup chopped green
    onion
½ cup sliced celery
1 cup julienne strips
    cooked meat (such as
    beef, ham, or tongue)
1 cup julienne strips
    cooked chicken or
    turkey

1 cup julienne strips
    Swiss cheese
1 can (2 oz.) fillets of
    anchovies, if desired
½ cup mayonnaise
¼ cup bottled creamy
    French dressing
Ripe olives
2 hard-cooked eggs,
    sliced

Have all ingredients chilled. Tear head lettuce and romaine into bite-size pieces; toss with onion, celery, meat, chicken, cheese, and anchovies, reserving a few strips of meat and cheese. Just before serving, blend mayonnaise and French dressing; toss with salad. Top with meat and cheese strips, ripe olives, and egg slices. *4 servings.*

TUNA ON A SHOESTRING

Ever make a salad with shoestring potatoes? We have! It's great! See it pictured opposite.

1 can (6½ oz.) tuna,
    drained
1 cup shredded carrots
1 cup sliced celery
¼ cup minced onion

¾ to 1 cup mayonnaise
    or salad dressing
1 can (4 oz.) shoestring
    potatoes
Crisp lettuce

Separate tuna into chunks; place in large bowl. Add carrots, celery, onion, and mayonnaise; mix gently. Cover and chill. Just before serving, fold in potatoes. Arrange in lettuce-lined bowl; garnish with parsley and carrot curls, if desired. *4 servings.*

"DUTCH-LUNCH" SALAD PLATTER

1 pkg. (10 oz.) frozen
    mixed vegetables,
    cooked and drained
1 cup cubed natural
    Cheddar cheese (about
    5 oz.)
½ cup sliced radishes
¼ cup chopped green
    onion
1 jar (2 oz.) sliced
    pimiento, drained

¼ cup dairy sour cream
2 tbsp. mayonnaise
1 tbsp. lemon juice
1 tsp. dill seed
1 tsp. salt
Crisp salad greens
Freshly ground pepper
½ lb. assorted sliced
    luncheon meats
4 hard-cooked eggs,
    halved lengthwise

In large bowl, gently mix cooked vegetables, the cheese, radishes, onion, and pimiento. Cover and chill at least 1 hr. Meanwhile, mix sour cream, mayonnaise, lemon juice, dill seed, and salt; chill. Just before serving, toss vegetable mixture with the dressing. Mound on salad greens in center of large platter; sprinkle with freshly ground pepper. Garnish with pepper rings, if desired. Arrange meat slices and hard-cooked eggs around edge of platter. *4 servings.*

CRAB LOUIS

4 cups bite-size pieces
    salad greens
2 cans (7½ oz. each)
    crabmeat or 2 pkg.
    (6 oz. each) frozen
    cooked crabmeat,
    thawed

4 tomatoes, quartered
4 hard-cooked eggs,
    quartered
Ripe or green olives
Louis Dressing (below)

Have all ingredients chilled. Arrange salad greens in individual large salad bowls. Drain crabmeat and remove cartilage. Top greens with crabmeat, tomatoes, eggs, and olives. Pour Louis Dressing over salad. *4 servings.*

LOUIS DRESSING

¾ cup chili sauce
½ cup mayonnaise
1 tsp. minced onion
½ tsp. sugar

¼ tsp. Worcestershire
    sauce
Salt to taste

Mix all ingredients; chill 30 min.

Pictured from top to bottom: Tuna on a Shoestring, All-in-One Salad, Bacon 'n Tomato Salad

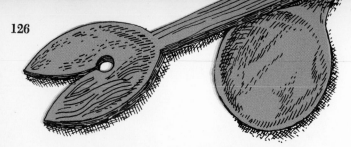

BACON 'N TOMATO SALAD

The popular flavor combination of a bacon-lettuce-and-tomato sandwich has been captured in this delicious salad. Pictured on p. 125.

1 head lettuce, torn into bite-size pieces	2 large tomatoes, cut into eighths
2 cups cubed cooked chicken	1 hard-cooked egg, sliced
8 to 10 slices bacon, crisply fried	Barbecue Dressing (below)

Have lettuce and chicken well chilled. Combine in a bowl. Break bacon into large pieces and lightly toss with lettuce mixture. Top with chilled tomatoes and hard-cooked egg. Serve with chilled Barbecue Dressing. *4 servings.*

BARBECUE DRESSING

½ cup mayonnaise or salad dressing	1 tbsp. instant minced onion
¼ cup bottled barbecue sauce	1 tbsp. lemon juice
	½ tsp. salt
	¼ tsp. pepper

Mix all ingredients; chill.

ALL-IN-ONE SALAD

Pictured on p. 125.

½ head lettuce, torn into bite-size pieces	½ medium onion, sliced
1 can (8 oz.) green beans, drained	¼ cup sweet pickle relish, drained, or ¼ cup chopped sweet pickles
1 tomato, cut into eighths	
1 cup cubed cooked pared potatoes	1 clove garlic, minced
1 can (6½ oz.) tuna, flaked, or 1 cup julienne strips cooked ham	2 hard-cooked eggs, sliced
	French dressing

Have all ingredients well chilled; toss together. *4 to 6 servings.*

FRUITED CHICKEN SALAD

3 tbsp. lemon juice	1 tsp. salt
4 cups cubed cooked chicken	½ tsp. pepper
1 cup sliced celery	⅓ cup mayonnaise or salad dressing
1 cup seedless green grapes, halved	¼ cup chopped almonds, toasted
1 jar (2 oz.) pimiento, drained and chopped	1 bunch romaine or leaf lettuce
⅓ cup finely chopped onion	1 cup cantaloupe balls

In medium bowl, pour lemon juice over chicken; mix lightly. Add remaining ingredients except romaine and cantaloupe balls. Toss until mixed; cover and chill. When ready to serve, line bowl with half the romaine. Tear remaining romaine into salad bowl. Spoon salad over romaine in bowl. Trim with cantaloupe balls. *6 servings.*

Betty Crocker Note: For a spectacular salad in a melon bowl, pile chicken salad in cantaloupe halves; omit melon balls and garnish with clusters of green grapes.

SALAD OF THE STATES

1 cup bite-size pieces head lettuce	4 large pimiento-stuffed olives, sliced
1 cup bite-size pieces romaine or escarole	1 grapefruit, sectioned (membranes removed)
½ cup bite-size pieces watercress	1 medium avocado, peeled and cubed
1½ cups cubed cooked lobster, crabmeat, deveined shrimp, or chicken	¼ to ⅓ cup mayonnaise
	Salt
	Crisp lettuce
½ cup chopped green onion and tops	4 large tomatoes, thinly sliced
	Parsley

Have all ingredients chilled. Toss together salad greens, seafood, chopped onion, olives, and grapefruit; chill. Just before serving, add avocado and mayonnaise; toss lightly. Salt to taste. Arrange the lettuce on salad plates; arrange 3 to 4 tomato slices on each plate. Top with salad. Garnish with parsley and, if desired, additional seafood. *4 to 6 servings.*

SUMMER SALAD BOWL

7 oz. uncooked elbow macaroni
2 tbsp. salad oil
3 tbsp. tarragon vinegar
1 tsp. minced onion
1½ tsp. seasoned salt
½ tsp. seasoned pepper
½ tsp. dry mustard
1 cup shredded natural Cheddar cheese
½ cup mayonnaise or salad dressing
1 cup cubed cooked ham
1 pkg. (10 oz.) frozen green peas, cooked, drained, and chilled
½ cup chopped celery
4 cups bite-size pieces spinach leaves or leaf lettuce
Paprika

Cook and drain macaroni according to package directions. Return to same pan; cover to keep warm. Mix oil, vinegar, onion, and seasonings; pour over macaroni and mix well. Add cheese, tossing mixture until cheese melts. Cover and chill. Just before serving, fold in mayonnaise, ham, peas, and celery. Line salad bowl with spinach leaves; spoon salad mixture into bowl. Sprinkle lightly with paprika. *4 to 6 servings.*

SEAFOOD SLAW

Hot corn muffins are dandy with this salad.

6 oz. macaroni, cooked and drained
3 cups finely shredded cabbage
½ cup chopped celery
1 green pepper, chopped
2 tbsp. minced onion
1 to 1½ cups cooked or canned seafood (shrimp, tuna, salmon, or lobster)
¼ cup salad oil
2 tbsp. vinegar
1½ tsp. salt
½ tsp. pepper

Combine macaroni, vegetables, and seafood in large bowl. Mix remaining ingredients; pour over macaroni-cabbage mixture and toss lightly. Chill 30 min. If a more moist, creamy salad is desired, stir in ⅔ cup mayonnaise. *6 to 8 servings.*

RAINBOW SHRIMP SALAD

Pictured below.

3 cups cooked rice
1 cup cooked shrimp, split lengthwise
¼ cup sliced celery
¼ cup sliced pimiento-stuffed olives
¼ cup chopped green pepper
¼ cup chopped pimiento
¼ cup minced onion
½ tsp. salt
¼ tsp. pepper
3 tbsp. mayonnaise
Crisp lettuce
6 cooked whole large shrimp, chilled
2 chilled tomatoes, cut into wedges
½ cup French dressing
Lemon wedges

Toss together rice, shrimp, celery, olives, green pepper, pimiento, and onion; chill thoroughly. Toss with salt, pepper, and mayonnaise. Spoon salad onto crisp lettuce; garnish with whole shrimp and tomato wedges. Serve with French dressing and lemon wedges. *6 servings.*

Betty Crocker Note: Crabmeat, lobster, or a combination of the three seafoods may be substituted for the shrimp.

PICNIC POTATO SALAD

4 cups cubed cooked
    pared potatoes
1 cup chopped celery
1 cup shredded carrots
¾ cup finely chopped
    onion
½ cup thinly sliced
    radishes
¼ cup bottled clear
    French dressing
¾ cup mayonnaise or
    salad dressing

1 tbsp. prepared mustard
2 tsp. lemon juice
1½ tsp. salt
¼ tsp. pepper
1 cup cubed cucumber
4 hard-cooked eggs,
    sliced
Crisp salad greens
½ lb. bologna, cut into
    strips ¼″ wide

Combine potatoes, celery, carrots, onion, and radishes in large bowl; toss gently with French dressing. Cover and chill several hours, stirring gently once or twice. Mix mayonnaise, mustard, lemon juice, salt, and pepper; add with cucumber and eggs to salad. Toss lightly and chill. Serve in large bowl lined with salad greens. Arrange bologna strips around edge of salad. *4 to 6 servings.*

CHEESE-POTATO SALAD WITH JULIENNE HAM

1 pkg. of our au gratin
    potatoes
3 cups water
1 cup water
1 tsp. prepared mustard
¼ cup mayonnaise

2 hard-cooked eggs,
    chopped
⅓ cup diced celery
1 cup julienne strips
    cooked ham

Empty potatoes into saucepan. Add 3 cups water. Heat to boiling. Reduce heat and simmer until tender, about 15 min. Rinse with cold water; drain thoroughly. Place in bowl; cover and chill. Pour cheese sauce mix into saucepan. Add 1 cup water and the mustard. Heat over medium heat until mixture boils, stirring constantly. Cover and chill. When ingredients are cold, blend mayonnaise into sauce. Combine chilled potatoes, the eggs, celery, and ham; fold in the sauce. Garnish with parsley and tomato wedges, if desired. *4 or 5 servings.*

SKILLET POTATO SALAD

The tangy German kind—easy with a packaged potato start!

4 slices bacon
6 frankfurters, quartered
1 pkg. of our scalloped
    potatoes
2¾ cups water

3 tbsp. wine vinegar
½ cup sliced green
    onion
1 tbsp. prepared mustard,
    if desired

Fry bacon until crisp in large skillet; drain on paper towels. Brown frankfurters in bacon fat. Remove from skillet; drain on paper towels. Drain fat from skillet. Empty potato slices and seasoned sauce mix into skillet; stir in water. Heat to boiling; cover and simmer 25 min., or until potatoes are tender. Stir in vinegar, onion, and mustard. Add frankfurters and heat through. Sprinkle with crumbled bacon. Garnish with additional sliced green onion, if desired. *4 to 6 servings.*

CORNED BEEF SALAD

Now here's a man-style potato salad! Corned beef, dill pickles, and potatoes—all tossed with a wonderful creamy dressing that just hints of horseradish.

4 cups cubed cooked
    pared potatoes
1 can (12 oz.) corned
    beef, cubed
½ cup diced dill pickle
½ cup chopped celery
¼ cup chopped onion
¼ cup salad oil
2 tbsp. wine vinegar
½ tsp. salt

¼ tsp. garlic powder
¼ tsp. freshly ground
    pepper
¼ tsp. monosodium
    glutamate
⅔ cup dairy sour cream
2 tbsp. horseradish
Crisp salad greens
Chilled tomato wedges

In large bowl, lightly toss potatoes, meat, pickle, celery, and onion. In a jar, shake oil, vinegar, salt, garlic powder, pepper, and monosodium glutamate until well mixed. Pour over potato mixture and toss. Cover bowl; chill 2 hr. or longer. Just before serving, mix sour cream with horseradish. Toss lightly with salad. Season to taste. Serve on salad greens; garnish with tomato wedges. *4 to 6 servings.*

HOT CHICKEN SALAD

2 cups cubed cooked
chicken
2 cups thinly sliced
celery
1 cup toasted ¼″ bread
cubes
1 cup mayonnaise

½ cup toasted chopped
almonds
2 tbsp. lemon juice
2 tsp. grated onion
½ tsp. salt
½ cup shredded Cheddar
cheese
1 cup toasted ¼″ bread
cubes

Heat oven to 450°. Combine all ingredients except cheese and 1 cup bread cubes. Pile lightly into individual casseroles. Sprinkle with cheese and remaining bread cubes. Bake 10 to 15 min., or until bubbly. *6 servings.*

TUNA-MACARONI BAKE

1 pkg. of our macaroni
and Cheddar
⅔ cup coarsely diced
celery
¼ cup sliced pimiento-
stuffed olives

½ cup water
½ cup mayonnaise or
dairy sour cream
1 can (6½ oz.) tuna,
drained

Heat oven to 350°. Cook and drain the macaroni as directed on package for range-top method except— after draining, combine with celery and olives in 1½-qt. casserole. In small saucepan, mix water and cheese sauce mix; cook over medium heat, stirring until thick and smooth. Stir in mayonnaise. Mix sauce with macaroni-celery mixture. Fold in tuna. Cover and bake 20 to 25 min. *4 to 6 servings.*

HOT CRABMEAT AVOCADO

Accompany with oven-warmed herbed potato chips and tall glasses of chilled tomato juice.

1 can (7½ oz.) crabmeat,
drained and cartilage
removed
⅓ cup chopped celery
3 hard-cooked eggs,
chopped
2 tbsp. chopped pimiento
1 tbsp. chopped onion
½ tsp. salt

½ cup mayonnaise
3 large or 4 small ripe
avocados
Lemon juice
Salt
3 tbsp. dry bread crumbs
1 tsp. butter, melted
2 tbsp. slivered almonds

Heat oven to 400°. Mix crabmeat, celery, eggs, pimiento, onion, ½ tsp. salt, and the mayonnaise. Cut unpeeled avocados in half lengthwise; brush cut surfaces with lemon juice and sprinkle with salt. Fill avocado halves with crabmeat mixture. Toss bread crumbs with butter; spoon over crabmeat mixture. Place in shallow baking dish. Bake uncovered 10 min.; sprinkle almonds over crumb topping. Bake 5 min. longer, or until filling is hot and bubbly. Serve at once. *6 to 8 servings.*

SUMMER SALAD PIE

Pretty as can be; pictured opposite.

1 pkg. (3 oz.) lemon-flavored gelatin	Dash pepper
1¼ cups boiling water	½ cup each chopped celery and pimiento-stuffed olives
1 can (8 oz.) tomato sauce	
1 tbsp. vinegar	¼ cup chopped onion
½ tsp. salt	Cheese Pie Shell (below)
Few drops each Worcestershire sauce and Tabasco	Tuna Salad (below)

Dissolve gelatin in boiling water. Stir in tomato sauce, vinegar, and seasonings. Chill until slightly thickened. Fold in celery, olives, and onion. Pour into cooled Cheese Pie Shell. Chill thoroughly. Spoon Tuna Salad on top of pie. *6 servings.*

CHEESE PIE SHELL

1 cup Gold Medal Flour (regular or Wondra)	½ cup shredded sharp Cheddar cheese
½ tsp. salt	2 tbsp. water
⅓ cup plus 1 tbsp. shortening or ⅓ cup lard	

Heat oven to 475°. Mix flour and salt. Cut in shortening thoroughly. Stir in cheese. Sprinkle water gradually over mixture, 1 tbsp. at a time, tossing lightly with a fork after each addition. (If dough appears dry, a few drops of water may be added.) Gather dough into a ball. On a lightly floured cloth-covered board, roll out 1" larger than inverted 9" pie pan. Ease into pan; flute and prick pastry. Bake 8 to 10 min.; cool.

TUNA SALAD

1 can (6½ oz.) tuna, drained	Salt
1 tsp. lemon juice	Paprika
1 tsp. minced onion	Mayonnaise or salad dressing
1 cup diced celery	

Lightly mix tuna, lemon juice, onion, and celery. Season with salt and paprika to taste. Chill. Just before serving, drain and mix in just enough mayonnaise to moisten.

SUNNY MUSTARD MOUSSE WITH HAM SALAD

4 eggs	½ tsp. turmeric, if desired
1 cup water	
½ cup vinegar	¼ tsp. salt
½ cup sugar	1 cup whipping cream, whipped
1 envelope (1 tbsp.) unflavored gelatin	
	Crisp leaf lettuce or romaine
1½ tbsp. dry mustard or 2 tbsp. prepared mustard	
	Ham Salad (below)

Beat eggs in top of double boiler. Add water and vinegar to beaten eggs. Mix sugar, gelatin, dry mustard, turmeric, and salt. (If using prepared mustard, add to beaten eggs.) Stir into egg mixture; cook over boiling water, stirring constantly, until slightly thickened (about the consistency of whipping cream). Cool completely; fold in whipped cream. Turn into 1½-qt. ring mold. Chill until firm. Unmold on leaf lettuce or romaine. Fill center with Ham Salad. *8 servings.*

HAM SALAD

2 cups cubed cooked ham	½ cup mayonnaise
1 cup diced celery	2 hard-cooked eggs, cut up
1 tbsp. lemon juice	Salt and pepper

Toss ham, celery, and the lemon juice together. Stir in mayonnaise. Carefully fold in eggs. Salt and pepper to taste. Chill thoroughly. Pile in center of Mustard Mousse.

SALMON SUPREME

1 can (1 lb.) red salmon, drained and flaked (reserve liquid)*
1 pkg. (3 oz.) lemon-flavored gelatin
3 tbsp. lemon juice
½ cup mayonnaise
¾ cup finely chopped celery
¼ cup diced cucumber
3 tbsp. sweet pickle relish
2 tbsp. minced green onion
1 tsp. salt
Dash pepper
Romaine or other dark salad greens
4 hard-cooked eggs, sliced
1 lemon, cut into wedges
Ripe olives
Chilled plums, melon wedges, Bing cherries

Add enough water to reserved liquid from salmon to make 1 cup; heat to boiling. Pour over gelatin; stir until dissolved. Stir in salmon, lemon juice, mayonnaise, celery, cucumber, pickle relish, onion, and seasonings. Pour into 1½-qt. mold; chill until set. Unmold on platter lined with salad greens. Arrange egg slices, lemon wedges, olives, and fruit around salad. *6 to 8 servings.*

*Or use 2 cans (6½ oz. each) tuna, drained and flaked. Dissolve gelatin in 1 cup boiling water instead of reserved liquid.

JELLIED SWEDISH ASPIC

1 envelope (1 tbsp.) unflavored gelatin
¼ cup cold water
½ cup tomato juice
¾ lb. smoked liver sausage (Braunschweiger)
1 cup tomato juice
½ cup mayonnaise
2 tbsp. lemon juice
2 tsp. sugar
½ tsp. salt
½ tsp. dry mustard
⅛ tsp. pepper
⅛ tsp. cloves
¾ cup finely chopped celery
¼ cup chopped green pepper
¼ cup chopped pimiento-stuffed olives
¼ cup finely chopped green onion
Shredded crisp lettuce
1 chilled tomato, sliced
1 pkg. (10 oz.) frozen asparagus spears, cooked, drained, and chilled
2 hard-cooked eggs, sliced

Soften gelatin in cold water. Heat ½ cup tomato juice. Add gelatin mixture; stir until dissolved. Chill until partially set. Soften liver sausage by mashing with spoon; stir into gelatin mixture along with remaining ingredients except lettuce, tomato, asparagus, and eggs. Pour into loaf pan, 9x5x3". Chill until set. Unmold on lettuce; garnish with tomato slices, asparagus, and eggs. *6 to 8 servings.*

SUNBURST FRUIT PLATE

A delicate combination of colorful fruit.

Pineapple slices
Orange slices or sections
Sliced banana
Clusters of grapes
Melon balls and slices
    (rind cut off)
Strawberries

Curried Cottage Cheese
    (right)
Orange and lime sherbet
Crisp lettuce or leaves
Three-fruit Dressing or
    Lemon-Honey
    Dressing (right)

Have all ingredients chilled. Arrange fruit, Curried Cottage Cheese, and scoops of sherbet on lettuce-lined serving plate or individual salad plates. (If desired, substitute your favorite in-season fruit for any of the above.) Pass one of the dressings.

Betty Crocker Note: To prevent banana slices from darkening, dip in lemon juice or in an ascorbic-acid mixture.

CURRIED COTTAGE CHEESE

1 carton (12 oz.)
    creamed small-curd
    cottage cheese

¼ cup toasted slivered
    almonds
1 tbsp. mayonnaise
½ tsp. curry powder

Thoroughly mix all ingredients. Chill 1 hr. or longer. *3 or 4 servings.*

THREE-FRUIT DRESSING

½ cup sugar
1½ tbsp. cornstarch
½ cup unsweetened
    pineapple juice

Grated peels of 1 small
    lemon and 1 small
    orange
2 tbsp. lemon juice
2 tbsp. orange juice

Mix sugar and cornstarch in small saucepan. Stir in pineapple juice. Heat to boiling, stirring constantly; boil 1 min. Remove from heat. Stir in remaining ingredients; cool. *Makes 1¼ cups.*

LEMON-HONEY DRESSING

⅓ cup frozen lemonade
    or limeade concentrate
    (undiluted), thawed

⅓ cup honey
⅓ cup salad oil
1 tsp. celery seed

Mix all ingredients in small bowl. Beat thoroughly with rotary beater. *Makes 1 cup.*

Whether a snack-size meal or a banquet on bread, sandwiches are all things to all men! A finger food, a juicy burger, an open-face sandwich to eat with knife and fork—such portable meals-in-themselves are at home in the kitchen, by the television set, at the fireside, or "on location" out of doors.

And remember, some of the most enjoyable parties begin with an invitation to "make your own" from a table lavishly laid with mix-or-match sandwich fixings of fresh breads in variety, delicious spreads, meats and cheeses, spunky mustards and relishes.

A WORLD OF BREADS

Good bread, the staff of life, is the basis of all these sandwich meals. The list of breads you may choose from is nearly endless—favorites from many countries, each with special flavor and texture to blend best with certain foods. Experiment to suit your family's taste with white bread you have made yourself, with onion or herb breads, Swedish rye, Russian caraway or pumpernickel loaves, crusty sourdough bread, English muffins, biscuits, rolls and buns in many forms.

TUNA CHEESIES

1 can (6½ oz.) tuna, drained and flaked	Butter or margarine
¼ cup finely chopped onion	8 rusks or 4 English muffins, halved
¼ cup chopped celery	8 slices tomato
2 tbsp. mayonnaise or salad dressing	8 slices process American cheese
¼ tsp. salt	Mayonnaise or salad dressing
¼ tsp. pepper	Parsley

Mix tuna, onion, celery, 2 tbsp. mayonnaise, the salt, and pepper. Butter rusks or muffins; toast under the broiler. Spread with tuna mixture. Top each with a tomato slice. Trim cheese to fit bread; place on top of tomato. Spread cheese with mayonnaise. Set oven control at "broil." Broil 5" from heat 3 to 5 min., or until cheese is lightly browned. Serve immediately. Garnish with parsley. *4 servings.*

CHICKEN SANDWICHES EN CASSEROLE

12 slices sandwich bread	2 tbsp. chopped pimiento
¼ cup soft butter or margarine	½ tsp. salt
2 to 3 tsp. prepared mustard	¼ tsp. pepper
2 cups chopped cooked chicken	1 can (10½ oz.) cream of chicken soup
1 cup shredded Cheddar cheese	1 pkg. (10 oz.) frozen green peas, slightly thawed and broken apart
⅓ cup finely chopped onion	

Heat oven to 350°. Trim crusts from bread. Blend butter and mustard; spread on bread. Arrange 6 slices of bread, buttered side up, in oblong baking dish, 11½x7½x1½". Combine chicken, cheese, onion, pimiento, salt, and pepper. Spread chicken mixture evenly over bread slices in baking dish. Cut remaining 6 slices bread in half diagonally; arrange over filling, buttered side up. Combine soup and peas. Spoon over and around sandwiches. Bake 25 to 30 min., or until center is hot. Lift out sandwiches to serve. *6 servings.*

HOT 'N ZIPPY SANDWICH LOAF

Pictured above.

1 loaf (1 lb.) unsliced white bread (about 8″ long)
½ cup soft butter or margarine
3 tbsp. instant minced onion
3 tbsp. prepared mustard
1 tbsp. poppy seed
1 tbsp. lemon juice
Dash cayenne pepper
12 slices Swiss cheese
12 thin slices large salami
Tomato wedges
Cucumber slices

Heat oven to 350°. Lightly grease a baking sheet. Carefully slice crusts from bread. Make 6 diagonal cuts, at equal intervals, from top almost through to bottom of loaf. Place on baking sheet. Mix thoroughly butter, onion, mustard, poppy seed, lemon juice, and cayenne pepper. Reserve about 3 tbsp. of this mixture and set aside. With small spatula, spread remaining mixture between cuts. Alternate 2 cheese slices and 2 salami slices in each cut, allowing each to stick out slightly at top and sides of bread. Spread reserved butter mixture over top and sides of loaf. Bake 25 min., or until cheese melts and loaf is lightly browned. To serve, remove loaf with wide spatulas onto a serving plate. With sharp knife, slice through each diagonal cut. Arrange tomato wedges and cucumber slices on plate. Garnish with parsley, if desired. *6 servings.*

ASPARAGUS SANDWICH PUFF

Just the specialty for a spring luncheon.

1 lb. fresh asparagus*
6 slices sandwich bread
Soft butter or margarine
2 eggs, separated
1 tsp. lemon juice
½ cup mayonnaise
½ tsp. dill seed
½ tsp. onion juice or ¾ tsp. onion powder
¼ tsp. salt
2 large tomatoes, sliced and well drained
6 slices sharp natural Cheddar cheese

Heat oven to 500°. Wash asparagus and break off tough ends; cook upright in boiling salted water in deep covered pan 10 to 20 min., or until tender. Drain well. Place bread on baking sheet and toast in oven about 2 min. on each side, or until lightly browned. (Do not overbrown or toast will become tough and dry.) Spread toast with butter.

Reduce oven temperature to 350°. Combine egg whites and lemon juice; beat until stiff peaks form. Beat egg yolks slightly and stir in mayonnaise, dill seed, onion juice, and salt; fold into egg whites. Place a tomato slice on each piece of toast and cover with a slice of cheese. Top with cooked asparagus. Spoon beaten egg mixture over each sandwich. Bake 15 to 20 min., or until golden brown. *6 servings.*

*Or use 1 pkg. (10 oz.) frozen asparagus spears. Cook as directed on package.

HOT BEEF SANDWICHES

4 individual loaves of
French bread (about
6" long)
8 slices cooked roast
beef

1 cup beef gravy
1⅓ cups shredded
lettuce
2 tomatoes, sliced

Set oven control at "broil." Split loaves lengthwise and toast under broiler. Place meat and gravy in saucepan; cover and simmer 5 min., or until hot and bubbly. Arrange ⅓ cup shredded lettuce on bottom half of each loaf. Top with roast beef and tomato slices. Dip cut side of top half of each loaf into the gravy; place over tomato slices. Serve immediately. *4 servings.*

MOCK STROGANOFF BURGERS

1 lb. ground beef
1 can (3 oz.) sliced
mushrooms, drained
¼ cup chopped onion
¼ tsp. garlic powder
2 tbsp. flour
1 tsp. salt
¼ tsp. pepper

⅛ to ¼ tsp. nutmeg
1 cup dairy sour cream
1 can (1 lb.) French-style
green beans, drained
(reserve ¼ cup liquid)
10 hamburger buns,
split and toasted

Cook and stir ground beef, mushrooms, onion, and garlic powder until meat is browned and onion is tender. Sprinkle flour, salt, pepper, and nutmeg over meat mixture; cook over medium heat, stirring until mixture is heated through. Stir in sour cream and green beans (with reserved liquid); cover and heat through, stirring occasionally. Serve in toasted buns. *10 servings.*

TOMATO CLUB SANDWICHES

12 slices sandwich
bread
2 medium tomatoes,
thinly sliced
8 slices bacon, crisply
fried

2 or 3 dill pickles,
thinly sliced
Mustard-Cheese Sauce
(below)

Remove crusts from bread; toast on both sides. For 4 sandwiches, place 2 slices tomato on each of 4 slices toast. Cover with second slice toast. Place 2 strips bacon and 3 thin slices pickle on second slice toast. Cover with third slice toast. Pour hot Mustard-Cheese Sauce over the top. Serve immediately. *4 servings.*

MUSTARD-CHEESE SAUCE

2 tbsp. butter or margarine
2 tbsp. flour
½ tsp. salt
¼ tsp. dry mustard

Dash pepper
1 cup milk
1 cup cut-up process
sharp American
cheese (about 4 oz.)

Melt butter over low heat in saucepan. Blend in flour and seasonings. Cook over low heat, stirring until mixture is smooth and bubbly. Remove from heat. Stir in milk. Heat to boiling, stirring constantly. Boil 1 min. Stir in cheese until melted.

TACO HOT DOGS

⅓ cup chili sauce
1 tsp. minced hot chili
pepper or few drops
Tabasco
5 frankfurters

5 frankfurter buns,
partially split,
buttered, and toasted
⅔ cup shredded lettuce
⅓ cup shredded natural
Cheddar cheese

Combine chili sauce and hot chili pepper. Drop frankfurters into boiling water; reduce heat and cook 5 to 8 min.; drain. Place frankfurters in toasted buns. Spoon chili sauce mixture over frankfurters. Top with shredded lettuce and cheese. Serve immediately. *5 servings.*

RACHEL SANDWICH

This ladies' version of the Reuben Sandwich is pictured below.

½ lb. sliced cooked turkey or chicken
8 oz. sliced Swiss cheese
¼ lb. sliced corned beef

12 slices rye bread, buttered
Almond Coleslaw (below)

Just before serving, arrange slices of turkey, cheese, and corned beef on 6 slices of bread. Spread about ½ cup Almond Cole Slaw on each sandwich. Top each with slice of bread. If desired, butter both sides of sandwiches and grill. Cut in half to serve. *6 servings.*

ALMOND COLESLAW

2½ cups shredded cabbage
½ cup chopped celery
¼ cup diced green pepper
¼ cup diced cucumber
3 tbsp. minced onion

¼ tsp. salt
Dash pepper
½ cup mayonnaise
2 or 3 tbsp. light cream
½ cup toasted slivered almonds

Combine all ingredients except mayonnaise, cream, and almonds. Chill. Just before serving, blend mayonnaise and cream. Toss dressing and almonds with salad.

REUBEN SANDWICH

Serve with mustard and pickles as pictured below.

1 can (1 lb.) sauerkraut, drained
¼ cup plus 2 tbsp. mayonnaise
½ lb. sliced cooked turkey or chicken

8 oz. sliced Swiss cheese
¼ lb. sliced corned beef
12 slices rye bread, buttered

Mix sauerkraut and mayonnaise; let stand ½ hr. Just before serving, arrange slices of turkey, cheese, and corned beef on 6 slices of bread. Spread about ⅓ cup sauerkraut mixture on each sandwich. Top each with another slice of bread. If desired, butter both sides of sandwiches and grill. Cut in half to serve. *6 servings.*

IVAN'S SANDWICH

12 slices dark pumper-	6 to 12 slices cooked
nickel bread	tongue, chilled
Soft butter	6 to 12 slices Swiss cheese
1 can (12 oz.) tomato	1 jar (2 oz.) caviar
aspic, chilled	12 to 18 anchovy fillets
Leaf lettuce	Bottled mustard sauce

Butter bread. Remove aspic from can and cut into 6 slices. Place leaf of lettuce on each of 6 slices of bread; top with cooked tongue, small leaf of lettuce, and slice of aspic. Place 1 or 2 slices of cheese on each remaining slice of bread. Spoon caviar down center of cheese slices; arrange twisted anchovy fillets over caviar. Serve two open-face sandwiches per person. Pass mustard sauce. *6 servings.*

SUB SANDWICH

Whether you call this sandwich a Submarine, Hero, or Poor Boy, it's good eating! Pictured below.

1 loaf (1 lb.) French bread	½ lb. boiled ham, sliced
Soft butter or margarine	½ cucumber, thinly
½ lb. salami, sliced	sliced
4 oz. sliced Swiss cheese	1 large onion, sliced
2 tomatoes, sliced	4 or 5 crisp lettuce leaves
Salt and pepper	3 tbsp. prepared mustard

Cut bread in half horizontally. Spread bottom half with soft butter. Layer the salami, cheese, and tomatoes on buttered bread, seasoning tomatoes with salt and pepper. Layer ham, cucumber, onion slices, and lettuce on top of tomatoes. Spread top half of bread with mustard; place over lettuce. Secure loaf with wooden picks or short metal skewers. To serve, cut into 6 sections. *6 servings.*

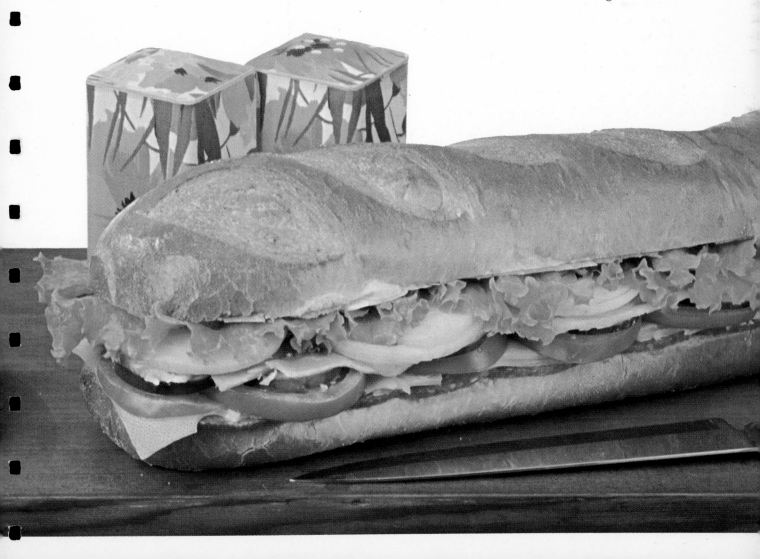

PARTY SANDWICH LOAF

Prepare fillings (below). Trim crusts from 1 loaf unsliced sandwich bread. Cut loaf horizontally into 4 equal slices. Spread one side of 3 slices with softened butter. Place 1 bread slice, buttered side up, on serving plate. Spread evenly with Shrimp Salad Filling. Top with second bread slice and spread evenly with Cheese-Pecan Filling. Top with third slice and spread evenly with Chicken-Bacon Filling. Top with remaining bread slice. Frost top and sides with Cream Cheese Frosting (below). Chill until frosting has set, about 30 minutes. Wrap loaf with a damp cloth and continue to chill 2½ hr., or overnight. *12 to 14 servings.*

SHRIMP SALAD FILLING

1 hard-cooked egg, chopped	¼ cup finely chopped celery
1⅓ cups finely chopped cleaned cooked shrimp	2 tbsp. lemon juice
	¼ tsp. salt
	Dash pepper
	¼ cup mayonnaise

Mix all ingredients.

CHEESE-PECAN FILLING

1 pkg. (3 oz.) cream cheese, softened	1 can (8¾ oz.) crushed pineapple, well drained
1 cup finely chopped toasted pecans	

Mix all ingredients.

CHICKEN-BACON FILLING

8 slices bacon, crisply fried and crumbled	1 tbsp. finely chopped pimiento
1 cup finely chopped cooked chicken	¼ tsp. salt
¼ cup mayonnaise	⅛ tsp. pepper

Mix all ingredients.

CREAM CHEESE FROSTING

2 pkg. (8 oz. each) cream cheese, softened	½ cup light cream
	Green food coloring

Mix cheese and cream thoroughly. Add a few drops food coloring to tint frosting a delicate green.

Good Cooks' Guide

A dinner in a dish can be only as good as the ingredients and preparation methods that go into it. In this chapter you'll find all you need to know to serve every meal in the book at its attractive and delicious best.

Because so many of these recipes call for cooked pasta and rice, chicken and shrimp, we offer here our latest "Kitchen-tested" guides for success in preparing them. You'll find other tips, too—ways of cutting ingredients, food equivalents, and facts about freezing. And whenever you're in a quandary about meal planning, turn to the recipes for salads and breads—all specially selected as perfect accompaniments to your one-dish dinners.

When your recipe calls for Rice that's Right

Because packaged rice is clean and ready to use, washing or rinsing is not necessary nor nutritionally wise. Cook rice in as little water as possible to retain nutrients, flavor, and texture. *Use a heavy saucepan, tightly covered, over low simmering heat to prevent moisture from evaporating and rice from scorching. Do not peek or stir.*

TO COOK RICE

1 cup uncooked regular rice	2 cups water
	1 tsp. salt

Combine ingredients in a 3-qt. saucepan with a tightly fitted lid. Heat to boiling, stirring once or twice. Reduce heat to simmer. Cover and cook 14 min. *without removing lid or stirring.* All water should be absorbed. *4 to 6 servings.*

For drier, fluffier rice: Remove pan of cooked rice from heat. Fluff rice lightly with a fork and let stand in covered pan 5 to 10 min. to steam dry.

For softer, moister rice (suitable for a rice ring): Start with ⅓ cup more water and increase cooking time 4 to 5 min.

OVEN-STEAMED METHOD

Use this convenient cooking method when serving large groups or when other foods on your menu are being prepared in the oven. This foolproof method will give you added confidence when it comes to cooking rice.

4 to 6 servings: Heat oven to 350°. Combine 1 cup uncooked regular rice, 1 tsp. salt, and 2 cups boiling water in 1½-qt. casserole or oblong baking dish, 10x6x1½″. Cover with tightly fitted lid or aluminum foil. Bake 25 to 30 min., or until liquid is absorbed and rice is tender.

8 to 12 servings: Heat oven to 350°. Combine 2 cups uncooked regular rice, 2 tsp. salt, and 4 cups boiling water in a 3-qt. casserole or oblong baking dish, 13x9½x2″. Cover and bake as above.

VARIETIES OF REGULAR WHITE RICE

Long-grain rice, favored by connoisseurs, is excellent for casseroles and combination dishes. It cooks light and fluffy; grains tend to separate.

Short-grain rice, less costly, is suitable for puddings and rice rings. It cooks tender and moist; grains tend to cling together.

RICE AND MORE RICE

To cook each of the following kinds of rice, follow package directions.

Precooked rice is dehydrated cooked long-grain rice, popular because of the speed with which it can be prepared.

Converted or parboiled rice is long-grain rice which has been processed to retain natural vitamins and minerals.

Brown rice, from which only the hull or husk has been removed, has a firmer texture and more nut-like flavor than white rice.

Wild rice, with unique flavor and texture, is really the seed of shallow-water grass from Minnesota marshes. Its kernels vary considerably in size and consistency.

Brown- and white-rice mixture or wild- and white-rice mixtures combine rice qualities to add interest of texture, flavor, and color to casserole dishes.

Seasoned converted rice packaged with prepared sauces offer convenience, speed, and interesting variety in flavor.

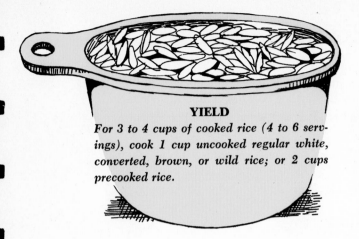

YIELD

For 3 to 4 cups of cooked rice (4 to 6 servings), cook 1 cup uncooked regular white, converted, brown, or wild rice; or 2 cups precooked rice.

Casserole Comments

RICE TIPS

To Keep Rice Warm: Rice is at its best when served as soon as cooked. If left in cooking pan for longer than 5 or 10 min., cooked rice packs together. When necessary to hold rice for a longer time, transfer it to a shallow baking dish; cover with aluminum foil and place in warm oven.

To Refrigerate or Freeze Leftover Rice: Cooked rice may be covered and refrigerated for about a week. Use in desserts, salads, casseroles, and soups. For longer storage, wrap in aluminum foil and quick-freeze. Frozen rice may be kept as long as 6 to 8 months.

To Reheat Cooked Rice: Use either of these two simple methods:

1. Heat cooked rice in double boiler over hot water about 10 min., or until rice is hot and fluffy.

OR

2. Place rice in heavy pan with tightly fitted cover. Sprinkle water over rice, using about 2 tbsp. water to 1 cup rice. Cover; heat over low heat 4 to 5 min., or until hot and fluffy.

To Make a Rice Ring: Lightly press 4 cups soft, moist cooked rice into well-greased 9″ ring mold. Keep hot until serving time. Unmold on hot platter. Fill center with creamed food.

For best results, use a baking dish or casserole of the correct size and shape called for in recipe. Too large a dish allows too much moisture to evaporate, leaving food dry; too small a dish causes food to bubble over. In too deep a dish, food will be undercooked; in too shallow a dish, it will be overcooked or burned.

A deep 1-, 1½-, or 2-quart casserole may be measured by volume. If you are in doubt as to its size, fill casserole to the brim with water, and note measure needed to fill.

A shallow baking dish is indicated in our recipes by dimensions, such as 10x6x1½″. To determine size, measure with a ruler across top from inside edges—first by length, then by width, and then from inside bottom to top for depth.

Never allow casserole or baking dish containing food to stand at room temperature. Dishes prepared ahead of serving time should be refrigerated or frozen until time to bake. Allow additional time for heating a chilled or frozen casserole.

When your recipe calls for Perfect Pasta

Noodles, macaroni, and spaghetti are often the basis of one-dish dinners. When pasta or rice is to be combined with other ingredients for further cooking, it is best to under-cook it slightly (*al dente*) rather than to overcook it. This helps to preserve proper eating quality.

Because pasta varies in size and shape, it is more accurately measured by weight in ounces than by cupfuls. When measuring less than a full package, carefully judge quantity by eye, subtracting from full package weight, or use the guide below for *approximate* cup measure.

MEASURING GUIDE

Allow about 2 ounces uncooked macaroni product per serving.
2 cups uncooked macaroni = about 8 oz. = 4 cups cooked = 4 servings
2 cups uncooked spaghetti = about 8 oz. = 4 cups cooked = 4 servings
4 cups uncooked noodles = about 8 oz. = 4 cups cooked = 4 servings

TO COOK PASTA

1 tbsp. salt **7 or 8 oz. noodles,**
3 qt. water **macaroni, or spaghetti**

Add salt to rapidly boiling water in deep kettle. Drop noodles, macaroni, or spaghetti into water gradually so that water continues to boil. (If spaghetti strands are left whole, place one end in water. As they soften, gradually coil them into kettle until submerged.) Boil uncovered, stirring occasionally, just until tender (6 to 10 min. or as the package directs). Test by cutting several strands with fork against side of kettle. Drain quickly in colander or sieve. Toss with butter to keep strands separate. Serve at once. *4 to 6 servings.*

EXTRA-EASY COOKING METHOD

Drop 7 or 8 oz. macaroni, spaghetti, or noodles into 6 cups rapidly boiling salted water (4 tsp. salt). Return to rapid boiling. Cook, stirring constantly, 3 min. Cover with tightly fitted lid; remove from heat and let stand 10 min. Drain.

Note: For thicker pasta, such as lasagne or kluski noodles, follow package directions.

TO RINSE OR NOT TO RINSE?

Rinsing washes away valuable vitamins and minerals and is not necessary if a good quality durum product is used. Rinsing in cold water should be done only when the macaroni product is to be used in a salad. It is essential then to chill the macaroni product to stop the cooking process.

TO COOK LARGE QUANTITIES

Use 2 tablespoons salt and 4 to 6 quarts boiling water for each pound of macaroni product. If more than one saucepot is needed for very large amounts, use the same proportion of salt, water, and macaroni product in each.

When your recipe calls for Cooked Shrimp

Shrimp range in size from tiny to jumbo. However, all species and sizes differ little in appearance and flavor when cooked and may be used interchangeably.

Since shrimp are very perishable, they should be used within a day or two after being purchased fresh from a reliable market, or kept properly frozen until used.

TO COOK SHRIMP

Shrimp may be peeled before or after cooking, as you prefer. For the easiest cleaning though, we recommend peeling and cutting the shrimp before cooking. Done this way, cooked shrimp has a pretty plump and ruffly appearance. For perfectly smooth cooked shrimp, cook before peeling.

PEELED-SHRIMP METHOD

1½ lb. raw shrimp in the shell, fresh or frozen	4 cups water
	2 tbsp. salt

Peel shrimp. (If shrimp are frozen, do not thaw; peel under cool running water.) Make a shallow cut lengthwise down back of each shrimp; wash. Heat water to boiling. Add salt and shrimp; cover and return to boiling. Simmer 5 min. Drain; remove any remaining particles of sand veins. Use as directed in recipe, or chill. Yield: ¾ lb. or 2 cups cooked cleaned shrimp.

UNPEELED-SHRIMP METHOD

Cook unpeeled raw shrimp as directed in recipe above except—increase the salt to ¼ cup. Drain shrimp and peel. Remove sand veins. Rinse shrimp and use in recipe as directed, or chill.

SHRIMP YIELDS

For 1 cup of cleaned, cooked shrimp use:
¾ lb. raw shrimp in the shell
OR
1 pkg. (7 oz.) frozen, peeled shrimp
OR
1 can (4½ or 5 oz.) shrimp

HOW TO BUY SHRIMP

Uncooked—In the shell, either fresh or frozen; sometimes called "green shrimp." See cooking directions.

OR

Cleaned and frozen. Follow package directions for cooking time and method.

Cooked—Cleaned and frozen.

OR

Cleaned and canned, packed either in brine or dry, generally in 4½- 5-oz. cans.

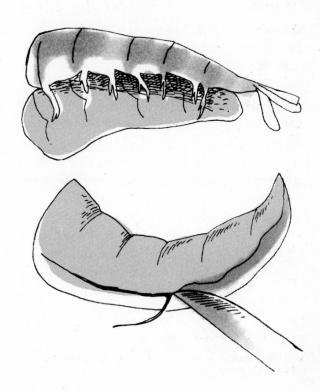

When your recipe calls for Cooked Chicken

Chicken one-dish dinners depend greatly on the flavor of the chicken itself. Well-seasoned, properly cooked chunks of chicken add much to the goodness of casseroles, skillet meals, and salads.

STEWED CHICKEN

A 5-lb. chicken yields 5 cups cubed cooked chicken and 3½ to 5 cups broth. A 7-lb. turkey yields 8 cups cubed cooked turkey and 5 to 6 cups broth.

4- to 5-lb. stewing hen or	**1 carrot, sliced**
5- to 7-lb. turkey	**1 small onion**
(with giblets)	**2 or 3 peppercorns,**
1 sprig parsley	**if desired**
1 celery stalk with leaves,	**Salt**
cut up	

Clean and cut up chicken. Place in kettle with giblets, neck, and enough water to almost cover the chicken (about ⅔ cup per pound of chicken). Add parsley, celery, carrot, onion, peppercorns, and salt (½ tsp. per pound of chicken). Heat water to boiling; remove any foam. Cover. Reduce heat and simmer gently until tender, 2½ to 3½ hours. To test the chicken, insert a fork into the thickest part.

Remove chicken and strain the broth. Refrigerate chicken and broth promptly in separate containers. When chicken is cool, remove the meat from skin and bones in pieces as large as possible. Skim fat from broth. Cover and refrigerate; use within 1 or 2 days. For longer storage, wrap and freeze (pp. 145-146). (If you know how the chicken will be used, you can slice or cube it before freezing.)

TODAY'S CHOICE—BROILER-FRYER

A 3- to 4- lb. broiler-fryer chicken yields 3 to 4 cups cubed cooked chicken and 2 to 3½ cups broth.

In today's market, broiler-fryer chickens are more available than stewing hens. Broiler-fryer chickens range from 1½ to 4 lb. Because they are young tender chickens, they require shorter cooking time. To stew a broiler-fryer, choose a plump 3- or 4-lb. one and cook as directed in the recipe at left except —simmer gently about 45 min., or until chicken is tender.

CHICKEN IN CANS
To speed up preparation time, call on convenient canned chicken.

Boned cooked canned chicken:
5-oz. can yields ⅝ cup cubed chicken
Whole cooked canned chicken:
3-lb. 4-oz. can yields 2½ cups cubed chicken

Freezing "Holdovers"

What a lovely feeling of security to open the freezer to a selection of your family's favorite home-cooked dinners in a dish, each ready to heat and serve at the end of a rushed day or when unexpected guests appear. To arrive at this secure state, double up when preparing recipes in this book—serve one recipe for dinner, freeze the other. Below are guides for packaging, freezing, thawing, and reheating casseroles and other meals in a dish.

COOKING FOR THE FREEZER

Prepare your meal in a dish according to the recipe except—cook for shorter time than recipe directs, as cooking will be completed during reheating time. Vegetables, rice, spaghetti, macaroni, and noodles should be slightly undercooked to prevent a too-soft texture and "warmed-over" flavor when reheated.

If only part of the recipe is to be frozen, remove it from pan before it is completely cooked.

Cool cooked food quickly to stop cooking action. To hasten cooling, set container in pan of iced water or directly on ice. Change water and add ice as needed. Wrap immediately for freezing.

Wait to add potatoes to soup and stews until reheating time to avoid grainy or mushy texture and "off-flavor."

When using pepper, cloves or garlic, season lightly as they may develop strong flavors.

Add ¼ tsp. monosodium glutamate to a family-size meal in a dish to help retain flavors.

PACKAGING FOR THE FREEZER

Use only recommended moisture-vapor-proof materials made expressly for wrapping foods to be frozen. Exposure to air during freezing causes deterioration and loss of moisture called "freezer burn," (food appears gray-white and shriveled).

Choose freezing containers of taste-free, odorless material in the proper size, and be sure they are completely clean. Freezing will not sterilize either container or its contents.

The best containers for freezing food are:
- Casserole or baking dish in which food will be reheated and served. (Flat casseroles that stack well are best for space economy.)
- Heavily waxed paper cartons.
- Glass freezer jars.
- Plastic or aluminum containers.
- Pliable wrappings of moisture-vapor-proof cellophane, plastic, or aluminum foil; plastic bags.

Fill containers at once with food that has been quickly and completely cooled. Allow ½ to 1″ air space at top of straight container or fill curved container just to "shoulder" to accommodate expansion of contents during freezing.

Pack food solidly, filling air spaces with gravy, sauce, or broth whenever possible. When using pliable material, wrap tightly, pushing out air pockets.

To hold solid food in stews and soups beneath level of liquid, fill the 1″ air space with crumpled freezer paper.

Seal with freezer tape all containers not equipped with airtight seals.

Label packages with name, quantity of food, and date, using china marking pencil, soft crayon, felt pen, or tag.

FREEZER STORAGE

Freeze food at 0° F. or below. Until food is frozen, place it in quickest freezing area or in direct contact with freezer walls or shelves, away from other frozen foods. Allow cold air to circulate around packages. Do not overload freezer by freezing too much at one time.

Maintain freezer temperature at 0° F. or below during entire storage period to preserve flavor, texture, and nutrients of foods.

Never refreeze thawed foods.

Packaged and properly frozen, these foods may be stored safely in your freezer.

To 4 months: Cooked meats and vegetables, stews, most precooked casseroles and skillet meals, chicken and meat pies, meat loaves, hash, soups, gravies, sauces.

To 2 months: Turkey pies, stuffings, chili con carne.

To 1 month: Fried foods, dishes containing macaroni, spaghetti, noodles, and rice, leftovers not frozen within one hour of preparation time.

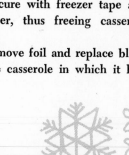

REHEATING FROZEN DISHES

Skillet meals, soups, or stews may be partially thawed in refrigerator, then reheated in heavy saucepan or skillet over low heat. Or heat in double boiler. Food should be heated to serving temperature and served immediately.

Frozen casseroles in oven-proof glass or metal may be placed directly in a heated oven. Or they may be thawed in refrigerator before reheating.

Length of reheating time required varies with temperature of food and size of dish. Food is ready to serve when it is bubbly hot in center.

PARTIES FROM THE FREEZER

Make the most of your freezer for party giving.

Make and freeze a party casserole from this book, following rules in this chapter.

Freeze party breads (either rolls made in advance or herb- or garlic-buttered French bread, wrapped in aluminum foil and ready for the oven).

Prepare dessert and freeze ahead of time—a frozen pie, a whipped-cream frosted cake, biscuit tortoni, or an ice-cream and fruit dessert.

On the party day, all you need prepare are the appetizer, salad, and coffee. What a marvelously easy way to entertain!

DISH-SAVING TIP

You may line a casserole with heavy-duty aluminum foil and freeze the food in it; then remove foil and contents, rewrap in more foil, molding it to food to eliminate air and closing it with a double-fold "drugstore" wrap. Secure with freezer tape and return to freezer, thus freeing casserole for daily use.

To reheat, remove foil and replace block of food in same casserole in which it had been frozen.

Cutting Cues

When your recipe calls for cut-up ingredients, chop, slice, dice, mince, or snip them neatly into uniform, attractive pieces like this:

1 DICE ONION
Peel onion; cut off end slice. Cut exposed surface deeply into tiny squares. Cut crosswise into thin slices, making ¼″ cubes.

2 CUBE VEGETABLES OR MEAT
Cut into ½″ cubes.

3 SLICE CELERY OR OTHER VEGETABLES
Prepare several stalks at once to save time. For pretty salads and Oriental specialties, cut celery into thin slices on the diagonal.

4 SLICE FRESH MUSHROOMS
Wash mushrooms gently; never soak. Trim off spots; cut off tips of stems. For attractive slices, cut whole mushrooms through stems.

5 JULIENNE STRIPS OF MEAT OR CHEESE
Cut in match-like strips.

6 CHOP OR MINCE INGREDIENTS
Chop on board with French knife, holding down point firmly and rocking blade vertically by handle, swivelling from side to side until food is cut into pieces of desired size.

7 MINCE PARSLEY
Cut or break off stem; snip washed parsley in glass measuring cup with kitchen shears.

8 SHRED VEGETABLES OR CHEESE
Rub on coarse part of grater over board, bowl, or waxed paper.

9 GRATE LEMON AND ORANGE PEEL, HARD CHEESE
Rub on fine part of grater over board, bowl, or waxed paper.

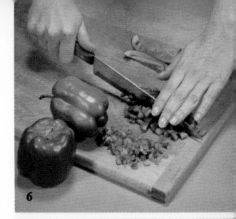

Equivalent Chart

Food	To Get	You'll Need Approximately
Apple	1 cup chopped	1 small apple
Bananas	1 cup sliced	1 to 2 bananas
Cabbage	1 cup shredded	¼ lb.
Carrots	1 cup shredded	1 to 2 carrots
	1 cup thinly sliced	2 to 3 carrots
	1 cup julienne strips	4 to 5 carrots
Celery	1 cup sliced	2 medium stalks
	1 cup diagonally sliced	3 medium stalks
Cucumber	1 cup diced	¾ of a medium cucumber
Cheese	1 cup shredded	4 oz.
	1 cup cubed	5 oz.
Cottage cheese	1 cup	8 oz.
Cream	1 cup whipping	½ pt.
	1 cup light	½ pt.
	1 cup dairy sour	½ pt.
Green pepper	1 cup chopped	1 medium green pepper
Lemon		
peel	1½ to 3 tsp.	1 medium lemon
juice	2 to 3 tbsp.	1 medium lemon
Meat, cooked	1 cup julienne strips	6 to 7 oz.
Nuts		
almonds	1 cup cubed	5 to 6 oz.
	1 cup chopped, slivered or diced	4 to 4½ oz. shelled almonds
peanuts	1 cup whole	5 to 6 oz. shelled peanuts
walnuts	1 cup chopped	4 oz. shelled walnuts
Onions	1 cup chopped	1 small onion
Onions, green	1 cup sliced	2 bunches (about 18 onions)
Orange juice	1 cup	3 medium oranges
Potatoes	1 cup cubed	1 small potato
Rutabaga and turnip	1 cup diced	⅓ to ½ lb.
Radishes	1 cup thinly sliced	12 radishes

MUSHROOMS

1 can, 6 or 8 oz. = 1 lb. fresh
    or
1 qt. fresh
    or
20 to 24 medium mushroom caps

1 can, 3 or 4 oz. = ½ lb. fresh
    or
1 pt. fresh
    or
10 to 12 medium mushroom caps

CAN SIZES

Size	Approximate Weight	Average Contents
8 oz.	8 oz.	1 cup
picnic	10½ to 12 oz.	1¼ cups
12 oz. (vacuum)	12 oz.	1½ cups
no. 300	14 to 16 oz.	1¾ cups
no. 303	16 to 17 oz.	2 cups
no. 2	1 lb. 4 oz. or 1 pt. 2 fl. oz.	2½ cups
no. 2½	1 lb. 13 oz.	3½ cups
no. 3	3 lb. 3 oz. or 1 qt. 14 fl. oz.	5¾ cups
no. 10	6½ lb. to 7 lb. 5 oz.	12 to 13 cups

Salads on the Side

Most dinners in a dish are so complete and satisfying that the simplest salad is often the only accompaniment needed. A tossed green salad, crisp and tart, is one of the best. Below is our favorite salad recipe, plus others for tossed salad variations and colorful molded fruit and vegetable salads.

BEST TOSSED SALAD

1 large head lettuce	**½ small bag spinach**
1 bunch leaf lettuce	**(2 cups)**
½ small bunch endive	**Classic French Dressing**
(about 1 cup)	**(below)**

Use choice part of greens; discard stems and cores. Tear greens into bite-size pieces (do not cut). Have them dry and cold. Before serving, combine as suggested with Classic French Dressing. *6 to 8 servings.*

CLASSIC FRENCH DRESSING

¼ cup olive oil (or half	**1 small clove garlic,**
salad oil)	**pressed or minced**
2 tbsp. wine or tarragon	**⅛ to ¼ tsp. freshly**
vinegar	**ground pepper**
¾ tsp. salt	**⅛ to ¼ tsp. mono-**
	sodium glutamate

Toss salad greens with oil until leaves glisten. Add vinegar combined with remaining ingredients. Toss again. Serve immediately.

ZUCCHINI TOSS

Crisp, distinctive, delicious. Perfect partner for an Italian dinner in a dish.

½ head lettuce, torn into	**3 green onions, sliced**
bite-size pieces	**(about 2 tbsp.)**
½ head romaine, torn	**1 oz. blue cheese,**
into bite-size pieces	**crumbled (about 2**
2 medium zucchini,	**tbsp.), if desired**
thinly sliced	**Salad oil**
1 cup sliced radishes	**Garlic Dressing (below)**

Toss the lettuce pieces, zucchini, radishes, onions, and cheese with salad oil just until leaves glisten. Then toss with Garlic Dressing. *6 servings.*

GARLIC DRESSING

2 tbsp. tarragon vinegar	**Dash each ground black**
1½ tsp. salt	**pepper and**
1 clove garlic, minced	**monosodium**
	glutamate

Mix all ingredients well.

FRESH MUSHROOM TOSSED SALAD

Choose large, fresh mushrooms for this salad.

1 head lettuce
1 bunch romaine
½ lb. fresh mushrooms,
washed, trimmed, and
sliced

Garden Dew Dressing
(below)

Tear lettuce into bite-size pieces; combine with mushrooms. Just before serving, toss with Garden Dew Dressing. Serve in bowl lined with romaine leaves. *6 to 8 servings.*

GARDEN DEW DRESSING

½ cup salad oil
¼ cup vinegar
¼ cup sliced green
onion
¼ cup minced fresh
parsley

1 tbsp. finely chopped
green pepper
1 tsp. sugar
1 tsp. salt
1 tsp. dry mustard
½ tsp. monosodium
glutamate
⅛ tsp. red pepper

Shake all ingredients well in a tightly covered jar. Keep covered in refrigerator. Shake well before using. *Makes 1 cup dressing.*

TOMATOES VINAIGRETTE

8 or 9 thick tomato slices
or peeled small whole
tomatoes
1 cup olive oil
⅓ cup wine vinegar
2 tsp. crushed oregano

1 tsp. salt
½ tsp. pepper
½ tsp. dry mustard
2 cloves garlic, minced
Minced green onion
Minced parsley

If using whole tomatoes, cut off tops. Arrange tomatoes in a square baking dish, 8x8x2″ or 9x9x2″. Combine the next 7 ingredients; spoon over tomatoes. Cover. Chill 2 to 3 hr., spooning dressing over tomatoes occasionally. To serve, sprinkle with minced green onion and parsley and some of the dressing. *8 servings.*

CELERY COLESLAW

1 tsp. salt
Dash pepper
½ tsp. celery seed
2 tbsp. sugar
¼ cup chopped green
pepper, if desired

1 tbsp. chopped red
pepper or pimiento,
if desired
½ tsp. grated onion
3 tbsp. salad oil
⅓ cup white vinegar
4 cups shredded cabbage

Place ingredients in large bowl in order given. Mix well. Cover and chill thoroughly. *4 to 6 servings.*

CUCUMBER RELISH MOLD

Like a molded relish—crisp and fresh flavored.

1 pkg. (3 oz.) mixed
vegetable-flavored
gelatin
1 cup drained shredded
pared cucumber

1 cup thinly sliced celery
3 tbsp. thinly sliced
green onion
¼ tsp. salt

Prepare gelatin as directed on package. Chill until partially set; fold in vegetables and salt. Pour into a 1-qt. mold or 4 to 6 individual molds. Chill until set. Serve with mayonnaise or dairy sour cream (thinned with milk), if desired. *4 to 6 servings.*

CRANBERRY RELISH MOLD

A favorite salad with chicken or turkey dishes.

1 pkg. (3 oz.) lemon-
flavored gelatin
1 cup boiling water
1 pkg. (10 oz.) frozen
cranberry-orange
relish

1 can (8¾ oz.) crushed
pineapple, undrained
1 unpared apple,
chopped
½ cup chopped celery
⅓ cup chopped nuts
Crisp salad greens

Dissolve gelatin in boiling water. Add fruit, celery, and nuts; stir until relish is thawed. Pour into 1-qt. mold; chill until set. Unmold on salad greens. *4 to 6 servings.*

...and Breads Besides

These breads score tops as partners for meal-in-one salads, soups and stews, or hearty meat-and-vegetable casseroles. When you're in a hurry, be sure to rely on one of our muffin mixes, refrigerated biscuits, or a Bisquick quickie to complete your dinner.

BISCUITS

2 cups Gold Medal Flour (regular or Wondra) °	1 tsp. salt
3 tsp. baking powder	¼ cup shortening
	¾ cup milk

Heat oven to 450°. Stir together dry ingredients in bowl. Cut in shortening with pastry blender until mixture looks like "meal." Stir in almost all the milk. If dough does not seem pliable, add enough to make a soft, puffy dough easy to roll out. (Too much milk makes dough sticky, not enough makes biscuits dry.) Round up on lightly floured cloth-covered board. Knead lightly 20 to 25 times (about 30 seconds). Roll dough or pat out to about ½" thick. Cut close together with floured biscuit cutter. Place on ungreased baking sheet. Bake 10 to 12 min. *Makes 20 1¾ " biscuits.*

CHEESE BISCUITS
Follow recipe above except—add ½ cup shredded sharp Cheddar cheese to the flour and shortening mixture.

CHIVE BISCUITS
Follow recipe above except—add ¼ cup minced chives to flour mixture.

HERB BISCUITS
Follow recipe above except—add ¼ tsp. dry mustard, ½ tsp. crumbled dry sage, and 1¼ tsp. caraway seed to flour mixture.

PEANUT BISCUITS
Follow recipe above except—add ⅓ cup chopped peanuts to the flour and shortening mixture.

°When using Gold Medal Self-Rising Flour (regular or Wondra), omit baking powder and salt.

BUTTER STICKS

Elegant, crisp, and buttery.

⅓ cup butter	2 cups Bisquick
⅔ cup milk	

Heat oven to 450°. Melt butter in oblong pan, 13x 9½x2". Add milk all at once to Bisquick in mixing bowl. Stir with fork to a soft dough. Beat 20 strokes. Dough will be stiff but sticky. Roll dough around on cloth-covered board lightly dusted with flour. Knead gently 8 to 10 times. Roll into rectangle, 10x6". Cut in half lengthwise. Cut each half into 12 strips (about 3x¾"). Dip each stick in the melted butter; arrange in pan. Bake 10 to 15 min. *Makes 24 butter sticks.*

MUFFINS

2 cups Gold Medal Flour (regular or Wondra)*	1 egg
¼ cup sugar	1 cup milk
3 tsp. baking powder	¼ cup salad oil or
1 tsp. salt	melted shortening

Heat oven to 400°. Grease bottom of muffin cups. In mixing bowl, stir dry ingredients together; make a "well" in mixture. In another mixing bowl, beat egg with fork; stir in milk and oil. Pour all at once into dry ingredients; stir just until flour is moistened. *Batter should be lumpy.* Do not over-mix. (When using Gold Medal Wondra, less mixing is necessary.) Fill muffin cups ⅔ full. Bake 20 to 25 min., or until golden brown. Muffins will have gently rounded and pebbled tops. Loosen immediately with spatula. Serve warm. *Makes 12 medium muffins.*

*When using Gold Medal Self-Rising Flour (regular or Wondra), omit baking powder and salt.

WHOLE WHEAT MUFFINS

Follow recipe above except—use only 1 cup flour and 2 tsp. baking powder. Stir 1 cup whole wheat flour into the dry ingredients.

CRANBERRY MUFFINS

Mix ¾ cup raw cranberries, cut in halves or quarters, and ½ cup confectioners' sugar. Let stand while mixing batter. Follow recipe above except— fold in cranberries with last strokes of mixing.

POPOVERS

A salad meal takes on added glamour when served with something hot—pass puffy popovers.

1 cup milk	1 cup Gold Medal
2 eggs, slightly beaten	Wondra Flour*
	½ tsp. salt

Heat oven to 450°. Stir ingredients together with fork just until smooth.* DO NOT OVERBEAT. Fill heavily greased deep custard cups ½ full or muffin cups ¾ full. Bake 25 min.; reduce temperature to 350° and bake 20 min. longer, or until deep golden brown. Remove from cups immediately. Serve hot. *Makes 6 to 8 popovers.*

*If using Gold Medal Flour (regular), beat all ingredients with rotary beater just until smooth. Do not use Self-Rising Flour in this recipe.

CORN MUFFINS OR STICKS

⅔ cup Bisquick	⅓ cup milk
⅓ cup cornmeal	1 egg
1 tbsp. sugar	

Heat oven to 450°. Combine ingredients. Beat vigorously 30 seconds. Fill well-greased muffin cups or corn stick pans ⅔ full. Bake 12 to 15 min. *Makes 6 muffins or 8 corn sticks.*

Betty Crocker Note: For quick and easy Corn Sticks, prepare our corn muffin mix as directed on pkg. except—fill corn stick pans ½ full.

QUICK CORN BREAD

Pictured on p. 16. Prepare our corn muffin mix as directed on package for corn bread.

To measure flour, dip dry nested measuring cup into flour; level off with straight-edged spatula.